MY BOOK OF WISHES

This book belongs to

_____

Dated

_____

Please give this book to

_____

Dedicated to

My beloved parents, James and Karen

May the love you gave so generously,

live on in all of us, always.

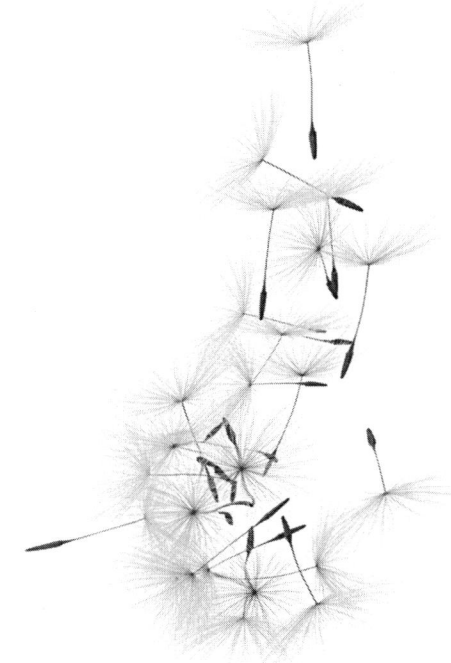

My Book of Wishes

The information in this book is based on the author's personal opinions and experiences. It is provided for informational purposes only and should not be considered a substitute for professional medical, financial, or legal advice. Readers are strongly encouraged to consult with a qualified healthcare provider, financial advisor, or other relevant professional before making any decisions regarding their health, medical conditions, or financial matters.

The author makes no representations or warranties regarding the accuracy, applicability, or completeness of the content and expressly disclaims all liability for any loss, damage, or risk—personal, financial, or otherwise—that may result, directly or indirectly, from the use of or reliance on this material. While this workbook may assist in preparation, it is not a legally recognized as a last will and testament. The reader assumes full responsibility for their choices and actions based on the information contained in this book.

Copyright © 2025 by C.J. Shearer
All rights reserved.

ISBN: 979-8-9986545-0-3 Hardcover
ISBN: 979-8-9986545-1-0 Wire-O
Book Cover Design by Sadie Stone
Printed by Kase Printing, Inc. Hudson, NH
Healthcare Proxy ©2016 Honoring Choices Massachusetts, Inc.

Manufactured in United States
First Edition

CONTENTS

INTRODUCTION — 7

MEDICAL AND VITAL GUIDANCE — 9
Recommended Supplies & Equipment – Homeopathic Suggestions – Healthcare Proxy

MEDICAL AND VITAL JOURNAL / LOGBOOK — 27
Record Your Current and Past Medical Information – Doctors – Insurances
Medications – Family History

WISHES UPON DEATH — 35
Details About Me and My Wishes – Death Certificate Information – Place for Photos

ALL ABOUT ME — 49
My Personal Preferences – What I Like and Do Not; Food, Comfort, Entertainment

MY FINAL WISHES — 55
Burial or Cremation Information – Service Instructions – Organ Donation

DEPENDENTS; INCLUDING PETS — 61
Care and Guardianship for Minor Children, Dependents, and Pets

INSURANCE — 67
All Types, Including: Medical – Life – Home and Property – Liability – Umbrella
Auto and Equipment – Business

PROPERTY AND ASSETS — 75
Real Estate – Rentals – Service and Maintenance Providers – Digital Activity
and Social Media – All My Stuff and What to Do with It

FINANCIAL — 97
Bank Institutions – Logins & Passwords – Investments Accounts – Trusts and Wills

FINANCIAL OVERVIEW — 113
Monthly Income – Expenses – Debts and Liabilities – Credit Card Information

LEGAL INFORMATION / IMPORTANT DOCUMENTS — 123
Power of Attorney - Healthcare Proxy – Will & Trust Documents
Driver's License – Passport – Birth Certificate – Marriage Certificate
Divorce Documents – Veteran Information (DD214) – Social Security

LAST WORDS — 133
Notes to Loved Ones – Apologies – Any Additional Notes

Introduction

Book of Wishes is here to help with something that most people would rather avoid — talking about and preparing for end of life. It is one of those topics we tend to tuck away in the very back of our minds, behind grocery lists, vacation plans, and remembering where we parked the car.

We all know that one day our time will come, but most of us treat it as though it is scheduled for the distant future, on a calendar we have not even bought yet. Whether we are reaching our golden years or facing health challenges, we often choose to believe that we still have plenty of time. Life can be like an ice cream cone on a hot day. Distracted by how good it is, but then melting faster than you can keep up with.

Having conversations about these topics are not easy. They ask us to sit with emotions we would rather not unpack. It is no surprise that many people choose to stay silent, hoping their legal documents or a few conversations will somehow be enough.

Perhaps you have already met with an attorney. Perhaps you have written a will, set up a trust, and listed who gets what, from heirlooms to houseplants. That is a great start. But even with all of that in place, many people still feel a quiet sense of uncertainty, as if there is more to be said, and more to be shared.

That is what this book is for. It is a space for wishes, thoughts, and personal touches that go beyond. It invites us to think ahead with grace, honesty, and maybe even a little humor. Because if we can laugh about it just a little, it might make the conversation a whole lot easier.

Now, take a moment to picture yourself seated in a chair, unable to express your preferences. Imagine the frustration of not being able to convey that you love spicy food, but all you are given is bland and unappetizing. Your caregiver, trying their best, struggles alongside you at mealtimes as you both navigate the challenges of communication.

Or maybe just imagine a scenario where they play classical music all day, believing it to be calming. What you really want is the upbeat pop songs that always made you smile. Hours pass, you find yourself feeling restless and disconnected, wishing you could simply express your desire for something different. The struggle to convey such a simple preference leaves you feeling isolated and frustrated. Do you know what happens to a still mind? I do!

I was my father's caregiver for four years and his assistant for a few years prior to that. I watched him slowly succumb to the symptoms of Parkinson's disease. We never really talked about his final days. It was too heartbreaking. I clung to the illusion that if we never spoke of it, he would somehow live forever. Staying positive and acting like nothing was wrong, made it feel true. Looking back, I regret not using that time to ask the simple questions that I would one day need answers to. I was constantly torn between my desire to make his final days as meaningful as possible, and the quiet heartbreak of knowing they were slipping away.

You could experience another type of scenario like our family did when my sixty-year-old mother passed suddenly, and without warning. The was no time for questions. No chance for closure. Just a long list of decisions and no idea what she would have wanted. We were heartbroken and overwhelmed, sitting in a consultation with the funeral director, being asked question after question. Every choice felt like a guess. And every guess came with guilt.

Unless you live alone on a deserted island, someone will be caring for you. Could be one of your children, a neighbor, a hired caregiver, or a nursing facility, but you will be cared for at some level by someone. That someone needs to know all these things about you.

Each section of this book offers ideas, checklists, and helpful examples — from practical to deeply personal. It offers some insight and shared experiences you may have never even thought about. I have included both legal and personal forms you can fill out and keep in this workbook. This book is your customized manual – your voice - your wishes – your story – all in one central location.

Inside, you will find charts, tips, and even a few tricks — not just for your caregivers, but for you too. It is a guide to help you navigate, express, and document your wishes for the now as well as prepare for the unknown. You gain clarity and a sense of peace. It becomes the Perfect Gift for you and your loved ones.

Medical Fundamentals

- ❖ **Current Medical Information**
- ❖ **Homeopathic and Supplements**
- ❖ **Allergies**
- ❖ **Past Medical**
- ❖ **Family Medical Information**
- ❖ **Footcare**
- ❖ **How to Prepare for Doctor Visit**
- ❖ **What to Bring with You**
- ❖ **Supplies and Equipment Guidance**
    - ○ **Tips, Tricks, and Suggestions**
- ❖ **Daily Health**
    - ○ **Vitals, Medication, and Hygiene**
    - ○ **Example Chart**
- ❖ **Healthcare Proxy**

MEDICAL FUNDAMENTALS

CURRENT MEDICAL INFORMATION

Your current medical information is one of the most important pieces everyone needs to know about you. Please make a list of all your current doctors, their expertise, and contact information. I cannot tell you how important this is. If they prescribe you medication, add the name, what the medication is used for, and the dose to the list. Are there any side effects? You could be taking a medication that has been working fine for years, but as we age, our body changes. Side effects could start to show up without you realizing it. They could even cause confusion that could be misinterpreted as dementia, but it is solely from a medication you are taking. If you or your caregiver witness this, reach out to the doctor right away. You must be your own advocate, be honest with the doctor, and be adamant. I have included a form at the end of this chapter that you can fill out, copy, and share with others.

HOMEOPATHIC CARE AND SUPPLEMENTS

Do you utilize homeopathic care, or vitamins and supplements? Put it on the list! There might be a day or incident that you had all this information tucked away in the everyday knowledge section of your brain with complete working recall. An unplanned sickness such as the flu or pneumonia could cause slight short-term or long-term memory loss and could affect your recall.

ALLERGIES

What are your allergies? Write them down! Many people are allergic to Penicillin. All your caregivers need to know if you cannot have certain medications. What if you are Celiac? Lactose intolerant? You know this, but it is not something you share with others on a regular basis. To the person caring for you, it could be critical; especially if you are rushed to emergency.

PAST MEDICAL INFORMATION

Your past Medical Information is equally important, and could affect your care. Make a list of any surgeries, any implants, who performed it, and when. Do you have a pacemaker, heart valve replacement, gastric bypass etc.? What brand of equipment is in your body, and what Doctor put it in. Having this list, is again, super important.

Why is this important? Let me share my grandfather's story. As he entered his mid-seventies, his body changed in ways he had not expected. Despite having a pacemaker put in many years earlier, he began experiencing alarming symptoms—racing heart, jitters, sleep disruptions, and breathing changes. It turned out, the unforeseen cause was that he no longer needed the pacemaker! It took some time to figure out, but others knowing your history, can save your life.

Again, be persistent with your medical team. It will be handy to have all that written down and easily shared with others. Every doctor asks you for it, so make a copy to bring with you. Imagine you passed out due to low blood pressure, your loved one is being grilled by the ER staff about your medical history. They mentally scramble trying to remember what and when you had procedures. What if it were a neighbor or co-worker, they most likely would not know your history at all. Write down your previous surgeries, procedures, any diagnosis's, dates, and performing doctors in the next section. This saves valuable time which could save your life.

FAMILY MEDICAL INFORMATION

What is your family's historical medical information? Was there diabetes? Heart attacks or strokes? Did your parents, grandparents, aunts, uncles, or siblings have any diagnosis' that your doctor might be wanting to know? There are many health problems than are hereditary, and having a quick log of that information can help you with your medical team in the future.

FOOT CARE

Footcare is more of a medical necessity than vanity or leisure luxury, and while I hesitate to add this information in the medical chapter, I struggled, and my dad suffered way too long to not include it. Health issues such as arthritis, reduced vision, and other conditions that limit mobility can make personal nail care extremely difficult, if not impossible. For those that might have toenail or foot fungus conditions, I am going to give you an alternative solution which could save you thousands of dollars, tons of time, and pain if it works for you, like it did my dad.

Toenail care protocol is to go to a pediatrist. Medicare will cover it, but not for the frequency you may need. Once I started driving my dad to his appointments, I would go into these doctor visits with him. My dad was soft spoken, and extremely tolerant, often finding it difficult to express his dissatisfaction. *(How he had a daughter so vocal and intolerant, I will never know)*

The Doctors job was to cut as much as possible, off his toenails. My dad requested multiple times that the nails needed to be filed smooth to prevent any sharp edges. These sharp edges would always catch on his socks, and made it near impossible to independently get them on.

Each visit was the same. Sometimes we left, and he was bleeding, and we never once left with smooth edges. His pleas for a cure were always dismissed or downplayed. The only advice the podiatrist ever offered was to buy sponges for his callouses, and try over-the-counter treatments for the nail fungus. None of these things ever worked. Let me be clear; he spent a lot of money, wasted a lot of time, and was incredibly frustrated — for over forty years! Not to mention, when a doctor accidentally causes an open wound, you are now dealing with the risk of infection — which for him, often triggered dementia symptoms or at the very least, significant pain.

We did finally leave that doctor and tried another, which was better. Then covid hit, and we were not allowed to go anywhere. They say blessings come from hardship, and because we were stranded, I found a company that specialized in hands and feet. They were called, "Footcare by Nurses." These nurses were miracle workers. Unfortunately, this group is only located in Central/Western Mass. Do some research, perhaps there might be a similar company that does the same thing in your area. Remember, a pediatrist is not a pedicurist, each has their own specialty, and as you age, you may need both! Regardless, let me share with you what those nurses did that cured (YES cured) my dad's toenail fungus.

- **Clip away any part of the nail that is easily removed**
- **File it, just like a salon or spa would if you had a pedicure**
- **Each morning, dab a cotton ball of white vinegar over each toenail**
- **Each evening rub feet down with organic coconut oil**
- **Once a week, soak feet in a vinegar bath**

This remedy is a natural and anti-fungal therapy. Keep your expectations of time realistic, if you stay the course, and are consistent, you will see amazing results in no time. May I also add that it was much cheaper than any of the pediatrist recommended over-the-counter remedies.

Hint -- Do not merge the two compounds to save time;
they will each offset the other, and you will not get the same results!

PREPARE FOR DOCTOR APPOINTMENT

This brings me to another important topic we must discuss in this medical chapter. You have cared for yourself, most likely your family, and probably many others during your life. You are no dummy by any means. However, as we age, it becomes increasingly difficult to retain, and sometimes comprehend what doctors are telling us during a doctor's visit. I am in my mid-fifties and find myself shaking my head up and down, acknowledging I understand what the doctor is saying. However, something typically happens between me walking through the parking lot *(noticing the bright flowers blooming)*, driving home *(dodging erratic drivers)*, getting distracted by a passing cloud *(that mimics a kid with an ice cream cone and zero coordination)*, or thinking of my never ending to do list. At some point, later in the day, someone will ask, "What did the doctor say?" I pause and try to unsuccessfully piece together the twisted details while hitting the key words of what I could recall.

I am sure we all have experienced a spouse or independent teenager go off to a doctor's visit on their own. After they return, you anxiously ask, "So what did the doctor say?" They respond with, "I do not remember," or "I don't know," or "Leave me alone, I am fine!" The last response most commonly coming from your teenager.

You as the patient typically get ten to fifteen minutes of the doctor's time, and in that period, you are having conversation, and trying to comprehend what the doctor is saying. Shortly, you are then either referred to a specialist, or given a diagnosis, with next steps forward. Not many people can retain or recall verbatim what was said during the whole visit. You are not a computer, so stop trying to turn yourself into one. Do not be angry when someone suggests having an additional person go with you; it is truly for your benefit. Two sets of ears are always better than one.

If you do not have someone that can come with you, or prefer to attend independently, my suggestion is to get yourself a little recorder. Life does slow down as we get older, and the world becomes a smaller place, but outside of our own space, the world is spinning at warp speed. Bottom line, you are responsible for your own healthcare, and need to be your own manager, and build your own posse. This will ensure nothing gets missed.

No one is truly paying attention to all parts of you, except you, and the people that care for you. We absolutely do have amazing and caring doctors, but they are doing their best in a very busy, over extended, somewhat broken healthcare system. Do not fall between the cracks.

WHAT TO BRING TO YOUR APPOINTMENT

- **Make a list of why you are going, with details and symptoms**
- **Write down any questions you might have**
- **Bring a copy of your medical history, and your current medications**
- **Have your recorder going during your appointment**

Using a recorder allows you to replay the visit which not only refreshes your memory, but also allows for note taking. It is amazing how much you miss what is said compared to a recording. Our minds wonder, or get hung up on their last response, and we become oblivious to the conversation in its entirety. Get a little recorder, and be prepared.

EQUIPMENT AND SUPPLIES GUIDANCE

Every time my dad faced a new limitation, I went on the hunt for a solution. I searched for anything that could help him stay independent or make life a little easier. Endless hours, often late into the night, with my nose buried in the computer, I searched for new innovative gadgets.

Let me share this with you—one of the *best* things you can have as you get older (besides a good sense of humor, and a snack stash) is a **combo leg and foot massager,** as well as a **heated hand massager.** These units make you feel like you are in heaven… or at least at a fancy spa.

As our bodies warranty runs out, keeping your blood flowing and tendons stretched is crucial, and these gadgets are like little personal wellness assistants. The hand massager prevented my dad's hands and fingers from curling inward. It gently flattened his hand out, and encouraged those fingers to stretch like they were reaching for the last cookie! Combine that with some heat and gentle pressure, and suddenly you will notice your arthritis pain minimizes.

We made it part of the daily routine every single morning. It became as normal as coffee and complaining about the weather. And hey… confession time; I bought one for myself too. Turns out, even *my* hands like a little spa day now and then. Who knew self-care could start at the wrists.

Once my dad progressed past the walker, the stabilizer belt, and reached a point where he could not safely walk from room to room; I was back on the internet looking for a solution. One thing I want to share and elaborate on is a handy little unit called, a **Sit to Stand machine**. This machine with brace included, can raise an individual from a sitting or lying position and set them down onto a bed, recliner, chair, or toilet. It is not a hoyer lift, (although it has the same premise) just nicer and easier on the person needing assistance. This type of machine can be used by one person rather than the hoyer lift needing two assistants. Bare in mind, the person in need must have the strength to stand. The brand we used was by BestCare, and it had handles for him to hold onto with assistance from the hydraulics to pull himself up. They make both a hydraulic and manual version. I was half his weight and opted for the hydraulic model. This machine helped my dad remain portable for an additional year and a half. Maintaining his routine and changing rooms throughout the day, brought him joy, *not to mention change of scenery.*

The other machine I bought at the beginning was a **hydraulic "Lift Seat."** This kept my dad independent for years. It works just like a recliner lift, but goes over the toilet. One of the most difficult challenges is to hold your body weight trying to sit down, or get yourself to a standing position. This little unit allowed my dad to keep his dignity and stay safe in the privacy of the restroom. I will include a list of tools that you may not even know existed in the further pages.

When it comes to equipment, not all has to come out of your pocket. Some can be covered through medical insurance, but most of it will come from other sources. Places you can reach out to are: your local COA (council of aging), and if your local COA does not have what you are looking for, reach out to your surrounding towns. You can also reach out to Churches, the Veterans, the Masons, and The French Connection. Check Facebook Marketplace, you would be surprised how much stuff has been previously purchased as new, and now no longer needed by other families.

For those that like lists, here are some supplies, equipment, and supplements you might find useful. Personally, I had to buy these out of pocket, but save your receipts for a possible tax credit. This list were things that worked for us specifically. There might be other items that you need or things on this list that do not work for you. Research, and do what is best for you.

- ✓ **Water bottles that measure ounces** – *Be mindful of how heavy they are when full*
- ✓ **Pill Sorter/Dispenser for a full week and time of day**
- ✓ **Reusable Bed Pads with handles** – *Buying these allow the skin to breathe, and getting ones with handles allows someone to adjust the person much easier*
- ✓ **Leg and Foot massager** – *What a terrific device that keeps the blood moving and helps with arthritis. Using the heat button is a bonus!*
- ✓ **Hand Massager** – *Same thought process as the Leg and Foot massager*
- ✓ **Chair Seat Cushion** – *When someone sits for a long time, it gives your toosh support*
- ✓ **Probiotics** – *Make sure you use a Probiotic with Pre-Biotics and Enzymes. Keeps things moving. The brand I found with a three combo was Shwartz brand; Amazon.*
- ✓ **Fruit and Vegetable Drops** – *Nutritional supplement; Amazon*
- ✓ **CBD Cream** – *Topical cream for aches and pains and inflammation; HempBombs.com*
- ✓ **Protein Additive** – *ProT Gold Brand is what we used*

- ✓ **Hydration Additive** – *It is very difficult to drink the amount of water needed. Adding flavor helps. We used Melaleuca brand because I could trust what was in it. I bought another brand from the grocery store and noticed my dad's blood pressure go through the roof, so be careful of the sodium content.*

- ✓ **Blood Pressure Machine** – *They do go bad, check on it periodically and have it calibrated*

- ✓ **Pulse Oximeter** – *Checks oxygen*

- ✓ **Voice recorder** – *For Doctor appointments*

- ✓ **Stabilizer Belt** – *Easily aids a second person to assist someone walking*

- ✓ **Vinegar and Coconut Oil** – *See the section I talk about foot care*

- ✓ **Apple Cider Vinegar** – *Great supplement. Research all its medicinal qualities; pill form*

- ✓ **Sit to Stand Machine** – *See in previous discussion earlier*

- ✓ **Toilet "Lift"** – *See in previous discussion earlier*

- ✓ **Rolling Tray** – *Check with your local COA or church for a possible loaner*

- ✓ **Portable Commode** – *Check with your local COA or church for a possible loaner*

Tips, Tricks, and Suggestions

Get yourself a **pill case**, one that is labeled Morning, Lunch, Dinner, Bed time or a version like it. Get it for 7 days a week. This is to be filled by you or maybe eventually a caregiver, once a week. It is easy to forget, even as a caregiver, so using this is super helpful and you will not be left wondering if you took your pill out of habit, or missed it. Screwing up medication or forgetting to take it can cause confusion, be diligent with it. Fill it on the same day each week.

Purchase two or three **water bottles** with ounces, and time of day along the side. I cannot stress the importance of drinking enough water! Number one sign of mis-diagnosed dementia and cause of UTI's, is lack of water. My dad's doctor told us he should be drinking sixty ounces per day. I have heard that you are to drink half your body weight in ounces. I almost fell over hearing this, but she was right! We found that ninety ounces was his perfect number. He was lucid, no UTI's, and regular bowel movements. If you do not like plain water, then get something to add to it, (just watch out for sodium levels). Listen to your body, you can flood yourself with too much, just as easily. Find your number. Surprisingly, eight or sixteen ounces. is not even close!

We used a lot of natural remedies. Look into **Apple Cider Vinegar**, seems to do so many medicinal things, and you can get the pill version from Amazon. No awful taste! **Pro and Prebiotics with enzymes** was a daily supplement in our cabinet. If the body struggles to get things moving, I suggest trying that first, before you reach for hard laxatives. Always check for drug interactions. Even Citrus juice and fruits cannot be taken with certain medications.

Cold Medicine can create confusion or even agitation. Originally, we used an over-the-counter cold tablet with my dad. My priority was to keep his sinuses clear and dry during allergy season (avoided down the road pneumonia). I had no idea that as you age, your tolerance changes. At one time he could take the recommended adult dose, but then I noticed the recommended dose of cold or allergy tablets created extreme confusion. The last couple years we used children's doses, and in addition invested in a high dose of **Manuka honey**. Research that too, and have it handy. I bought it from Amazon. A minimum of 700's+ MGO is what we considered medicinal levels. I am not a professional, but it proved extremely beneficial to my family, without side effects.

One of the top natural wound healers or wound preventors is consuming high Proteins. It is so difficult to get the required percentages in our bodies, especially as we age. I found several good companies that sold a **Protein concentrate**. Mix it into a shake or however you want to do it, but do it! We used a medical grade concentrate called, ProT Gold Liquid Collagen Protein. You can also get **Boost Protein Max 30g**. Maybe you are one that struggles to keep good nutritional calories. We used, Boost High Calorie Supplement drink.

DAILY HEALTH – VITALS, MEDICATION, AND HYGIENE

There may come a day that you need to start jotting things down for yourself, or maybe your loved one. At some point it could be critical to have certain information recorded daily. I added a general list, but I will also include the chart we used which you can copy. For us, each shift (morning, afternoon, and evening) filled it out. Anyone walking into his house knew his medical, vital, and hygiene health. If you live alone, and monitor your own health, make a list for yourself. Remember that we all forget, and you always need to be aware of your baseline. These questions are critical to medical staff if you were to be found unconscious or unresponsive. Putting this information down on paper or creating a medical journal makes it accessible and easier for others to see.

- **Temperature and Time Taken**
- **B/P and Time Taken**
- **Total Fluids Consumed?**
- **What Medication Taken and Time?**
- **What Supplements Taken and Time?**
- **Any Antibiotics Taken?**
- **Urine expelled, how many times per day? Was urine bright yellow without odor?**
- **Did a BM occur? AND has it been more than 24 hours without a BM?**
- **What and how much was eaten for each meal?**

Hint – Making notes in your phone or computer does not do anyone any good if a critical moment occurs. Having a notebook or binder was also handy to have, and look back on.

Here is the actual chart we used. Fluctuation in urine color or clarity could signal UTI. Recording Bowel Movements – You can get backed up after days which creates pain and could become a medical issue if left untreated. This is just what I used to communicate between all of us, feel free to customize it to your needs. I could fit two of these on one page.

Caregiver: _____ **Date:** _____

Total ML of Urine in Bag 8:00am _____ 7:30pm _____   <u>Disinfect / Change out / Empty Cath bag</u>
(Circle)

Temp & Time: _____ B/P & Time: _____ B/P & Time: _____
(Normal Baseline BP 115/75 Temp: 97.5)

BM & Time_____ Over 24hrs without bowel movement? YES   or   NO

****Did you give ex-lax or suppository? If yes, what and what time_____

(**Medications were located in daily container, it didn't need a check off, it was done every shift)

TOTAL Consumed Ounces during shift _____ (AM 40oz Lunch 24oz PM 24oz)

Did he need Amlodipine for Blood Pressure? Time_____

Was antibiotics given? _____Time_____

Did you give Manuka Honey? Yes   or   No

Did he have Shower or Sponge bath? (Circle) Shave? _____ Yes/No (Circle)

What did he eat for Meal? _____

**ANY Tylenol or cough syrup given? (Circle) Time_____
   **ANY Allergy tablet given? What was given and Time? _____

End of Day *** Please total oz of fluid consumed for the day_____ Total ML in bag_____

NOTES/UPDATES:

HEALTH CARE PROXY

Now we are going to talk about another extremely important must have document. You need to have a healthcare proxy. This is different than a Power of Attorney. A Power of Attorney handles your financial matters whereas a Healthcare Proxy handles medical decisions in the event you are unable to do so. This form is easy to get, most doctors' offices, hospitals, and attorneys have a form. You could also most likely go to the internet and download one. A Healthcare Proxy is a legal document that designates another person the right to not only your medical information, but in the event, you cannot make decisions for yourself, they can! I am including an example from my state of Massachusetts. Please make sure this would be valid in your state.

Naming your healthcare proxy is important. You want to choose someone that knows your wishes, knows you, and shares the same beliefs as yourself. Maybe it is your spouse or your children, or a dear friend. You can have multiple people be your healthcare proxy. My father had all three of us kids, but I was the one that needed it when talking to his doctors, working out medications etc. It gives your caregiver (family or friend) clout when advocating on your behalf.

Communicating your detailed wishes to your loved ones, and your caregivers is very important. The last thing you want is to have different opinions or hurt feelings flying around a room when your care needs to be the priority. Be clear, and trust the person (s) that you choose will have your best interest, and will follow your wishes as you have communicated. These details are not anything anyone wants to talk about, but you need to be clear and your wishes should be written down, and witnessed. Here are a couple of situations to think about—

Scenario one: You are in a coma, there is no chance you are coming out of it, and you need a feeding tube to stay alive. Do you want to continue life? Some people do, some do not, but it is a personal call, and it is better to make that clear *before* your family is left making decisions in panic or guilt mode.

Scenario two: You are sick, maybe have a fever, you are dehydrated, and non-responsive. Sounds scary, but you might just need some fluids and antibiotics. Simple, right? You would be surprised how often medical staff hesitates to treat someone in that state; especially older adults.

We experienced this more times than I can count. My dad would get sick, and every time it was the same symptoms: fever, confused, sleepy and barely responsive. The hospital emergency room staff or hospice staff would come in, look at him, and start wondering out loud if they should treat him. Wait, what? Yes, hospice or the emergency room view things differently.

Meanwhile, I am standing there like, "Umm… of course treat him, why wouldn't you? He is just dried out like a raisin, get the man some fluids!" You would not believe how much I would have to fight for this. They all were ready to sign his death certificate, and that was horrifying.

Sure enough, after a round of antibiotics and some hydration, he would bounce back like a spring chicken. (Okay, maybe more like a slightly tired chicken, but still—*alive and well!*)

So yes, some questions may seem silly at first, but they are very real. That is why it is important to have these very specific conversations early, write things down, and make sure your loved ones and care team are all on the same page. Remember, there is a difference from being in a coma that you will not come out of, or just being sick, dehydrated, even non-responsive. Be clear at what level you want to be treated.

The emergency room does not know your loved one's baseline, and Hospice is, unfortunately, known for stepping back when someone reaches this state, so caregivers often need to advocate firmly. Just so you know, being on Hospice for a terminal illness does not mean you cannot receive treatment for temporary issues, like a UTI or infection. Antibiotics are still an option. We will dive deeper into Hospice, through the caregiver's lens — in my next book.

Hint — The following two pages are an example of a Massachusetts Healthcare Proxy, it might be fine for other states, but please verify that. You can do a quick internet search to see if it covers what your state requires. I am also including forms to be filled out that helps you organize all your Medical Information we have been talking about in this section. Make a blank Copy in case things change, or write on a stickie over the section, which can be changed out.

Massachusetts Health Care Proxy Instructions and Document

Instructions: Every competent adult, 18 years old and older, has the right to appoint a Health Care Agent in a Health Care Proxy. To create your Health Care Proxy, print this two page form and place the instructions page and the blank document in front of you. Follow the step-by-step instructions and sign and date the Health Care Proxy in front of two witnesses, who sign and date the document after you.

1. Your Name and Address *(Required)*
Print your full name in the blank space. Print your address.

2. My Health Care Agent is: *(Required)*
Print the name, address and phone numbers of your Health Care Agent.
- Choose a person you trust to make health care decisions for you based on your choices, values and beliefs, if you cannot make or communicate decisions yourself;
- Your Health Care Agent and Alternate Agent cannot be a person who is an operator, administrator or employee in the facility where you are a patient or resident or have applied for admission, unless they are related to you by blood, marriage or adoption.

3. My Alternate Health Care Agent *(Not required, but helpful to have an Alternate Agent)*
If possible, appoint a person you trust as a back-up or Alternate Agent, who can step-in to make health care decisions if your Health Care Agent is not available, not willing or not competent to serve, or is not expected to make a timely decision. Print the name, address and phone numbers.

4. My Health Care Agent's Authority *(Required)*
Here's where you give your Agent either the broadest possible decision-making authority to make "any and all" decisions including life sustaining treatments, or limit his/her authority:
- If you want to give "any and all" decision-making authority, just leave this area blank.
- If you do not want to give "any and all" decision-making authority, describe the way in which you want to limit your Agent's authority and write it down in the space provided.

5. Signature and Date *(Required)*
Do NOT sign ahead. Sign your full name & date in front of two adult witnesses who sign after you.
- You can have someone sign your name at your direction in front of two witnesses.

6. Witness Statement and Signature *(Required)*
Any competent adult can be a witness except your Health Care Agent and Alternate Agent.
- Two adults must be present as witnesses when this document is signed. They watch as you sign the document, or as another person signs at your direction, and sign after you to state that you are at least 18 years old, of sound mind, and under no constraint or undue influence.
- Have Witness One sign, then print his or her name and the date;
- Then have Witness Two sign and print his or her name and the date.

7. Health Care Agent Statement *(Optional)*
This section is not required, but it can help your doctors and family know the Agents you appointed have accepted the position. Your Agent(s) signs and prints the date in the spaces provided.

Important: Keep your original Health Care Proxy. Make a copy and give it to your Health Care Agent. Give a copy to your doctors and care providers to scan in your medical record so they know how to contact your Agent if you are ill or injured and unable to speak for yourself.

©2016 Honoring Choices Massachusetts, Inc. • www.honoringchoicesmass.com
This document may be reproduced in its entirety with the source and the copyright shown.

Massachusetts Health Care Proxy

1. I, _____ Address: _____,
appoint the following person to be my Health Care Agent with the authority to make health care decisions on my behalf. This authority becomes effective if my attending physician determines in writing that I lack the capacity to make or communicate health care decisions myself, according to Chapter 201D of the General Laws of Massachusetts.

2. My Health Care Agent is:

Name: _____ Address: _____

Phone(s): _____ ; _____ ; _____

3. My Alternate Health Care Agent

If my Agent is not available, willing or competent, or not expected to make a timely decision, I appoint:

Name: _____ Address: _____

Phone(s): _____ ; _____ ; _____

4. My Health Care Agent's Authority

I give my Health Care Agent the same authority I have to make any and all health care decisions including life-sustaining treatment decisions, except (list limits to authority or give instructions, if any):

_____

_____.

I authorize my Health Care Agent to make health care decisions based on his or her assessment of my choices, values and beliefs if known, and in my best interest if not known. I give my Health Care Agent the same rights I have to the use and disclosure of my health information and medical records as governed by the Health Insurance Portability and Accountability Act of 1996 (HIPAA), 42 U.S.C. 1320d. Photocopies of this Health Care Proxy have the same force and effect as the original.

5. Signature and Date. I sign my name and date this Health Care Proxy in the presence of two witnesses.

SIGNED _____ DATE _____

6. Witness Statement and Signature

We, the undersigned, have witnessed the signing of this document by or at the direction of the signatory above and state the signatory appears to be at least 18 years old, of sound mind and under no constraint or undue influence. Neither of us is the health care agent or alternate agent.

Witness One
Signed: _____

Witness Two
Signed: _____

Print Name: _____

Print Name: _____

Date: _____

Date: _____

7. Health Care Agent Statement (Optional):
We have read this document carefully and accept the appointment.

Health Care Agent _____ Date _____

Alternate Health Care Agent _____ Date _____

This Massachusetts Health Care Proxy was prepared by Honoring Choices Massachusetts, Inc.

Medical and Vital Journal

- ❖ **Current Medical Information**
    - Emergency Contacts
    - Allergies
    - Insurance
    - Conditions and Diagnosis
- ❖ **Specialists Contacts**
    - Type and Contact List
- ❖ **Medication and Supplement List**
    - Medication Allergy List
- ❖ **Medical History**
    - Diagnosis
    - Implants
    - Cosmetic and Dental
- ❖ **Surgery List**
- ❖ **Family History**

NAME: _____ **DATE OF BIRTH:** _____

BLOOD TYPE: _____ **GENERAL ALLERGIES:** _____

EMERGENCY CONTACTS

Name & Contact Info: _____

Name & Contact Info: _____

Name & Contact Info: _____

INSURANCE INFORMATION

1. Primary Carrier: _____ Member ID: _____

Subscriber Name: _____ Company: _____

Contact No. _____ URL: _____

2. Secondary Carrier: _____ Member ID: _____

Subscriber Name: _____ Company: _____

Contact No. _____ URL: _____

3. Pharmaceutical Ins. Carrier: _____ Member ID: _____

Pharmacy or Mail in Address: _____

MEDICAL CURRENT CONDITIONS / DIAGNOSIS'

_____	_____	_____
(Type/Reason)	*(Doctor Name)*	*(Date)*
_____	_____	_____
(Type/Reason)	*(Doctor Name)*	*(Date)*
_____	_____	_____
(Type/Reason)	*(Doctor Name)*	*(Date)*

SPECIALISTS CONTACTS

PRIMARY: _____
          (Dr. Name)   *(Name of Practice)*   *(Address)*

        _____
          (Phone)   *(Email)*   *(Patient Portal Url / User Name Password)*

PHARMACY: _____
          (Name)   *(Address)*

        _____
          (Phone)   *(Email)*   *(Patient Portal Url / User Name Password)*

HOSPITAL: _____
          (Name)   *(Address)*   *(Phone)*

CARDIOLOGIST: _____
          (Name)   *(Name of Practice)*   *(Address)*

        _____
          (Phone)   *(Email)*   *(Patient Portal Url / User Name Password)*

PULMONOLOGIST: _____
          (Name)   *(Name of Practice)*   *(Address)*

        _____
          (Phone)   *(Email)*   *(Patient Portal Url / User Name Password)*

GASTROLOGIST: _____
          (Name)   *(Name of Practice)*   *(Address)*

        _____
          (Phone)   *(Email)*   *(Patient Portal Url / User Name Password)*

ENDOCRINOLOGIST: _____
          (Name)   *(Name of Practice)*   *(Address)*

        _____
          (Phone)   *(Email)*   *(Patient Portal Url / User Name Password)*

UROLOGIST: _____
             _____(Name)_____   _(Name of Practice)_   _____(Address)_____

             _____
             __(Phone)__ __(Email)__   _(Patient Portal Url / User Name Password)_

ONCOLOGIST: _____
               _____(Name)_____   _(Name of Practice)_   _____(Address)_____

               _____
               __(Phone)__ __(Email)__   _(Patient Portal Url / User Name Password)_

RHEUMATOLOGIST: _____
                   _____(Name)_____   _(Name of Practice)_   _____(Address)_____

                   _____
                   __(Phone)__ __(Email)__   _(Patient Portal Url / User Name Password)_

OPTOMETRIST/OPHTHALMOLOGIST: _____
                                _____(Name)_____   _(Name of Practice)_

                                _____
                                __(Phone)__ __(Email)__   _____(Address)_____

DENTIST: _____
            _____(Name)_____   _(Name of Practice)_   _____(Address)_____

            _____
            __(Phone)__ __(Email)__   _(Patient Portal Url / User Name Password)_

ORAL SURGEON: _____
                 _____(Name)_____   _(Name of Practice)_   _____(Address)_____

                 _____
                 __(Phone)__ __(Email)__   _(Patient Portal Url / User Name Password)_

MEDICATION AND SUPPLEMENT/VITAMIN LIST

Any Allergies to Medication? _____

(Medication)   (Reason for Use)   (Prescribing Doctor)   (Dose)   (Strength)

_____
(Interactions or Special Instructions)   (Refill Location)

— · — · — · — · — · — · — · — · — · — · — · — · — · — · — · — · — · — · — · —

(Medication)   (Reason for Use)   (Prescribing Doctor)   (Dose)   (Strength)

_____
(Interactions or Special Instructions)   (Refill Location)

— · — · — · — · — · — · — · — · — · — · — · — · — · — · — · — · — · — · — · —

(Medication)   (Reason for Use)   (Prescribing Doctor)   (Dose)   (Strength)

_____
(Interactions or Special Instructions)   (Refill Location)

— · — · — · — · — · — · — · — · — · — · — · — · — · — · — · — · — · — · — · —

(Medication)   (Reason for Use)   (Prescribing Doctor)   (Dose)   (Strength)

_____
(Interactions or Special Instructions)   (Refill Location)

— · — · — · — · — · — · — · — · — · — · — · — · — · — · — · — · — · — · — · —

(Medication)   (Reason for Use)   (Prescribing Doctor)   (Dose)   (Strength)

_____
(Interactions or Special Instructions)   (Refill Location)

— · — · — · — · — · — · — · — · — · — · — · — · — · — · — · — · — · — · — · —

(Medication)   (Reason for Use)   (Prescribing Doctor)   (Dose)   (Strength)

_____
(Interactions or Special Instructions)   (Refill Location)

(Supplement)   (Reason for Use)   (Dose)   (Strength)

_____
(Interactions or Special Instructions)   (Purchased from)

- -

_____
(Supplement)   (Reason for Use)   (Dose)   (Strength)

_____
(Interactions or Special Instructions)   (Purchased from)

- -

_____
(Supplement)   (Reason for Use)   (Dose)   (Strength)

_____
(Interactions or Special Instructions)   (Purchased from)

MEDICAL HISTORY

PREVIOUS MEDICAL DIAGNOSIS'

Date of Diagnosis: _____ Treatment: _____

_____
(Type/Reason)   (Doctor Name)   (Date Cleared)

Date of Diagnosis: _____ Treatment: _____

_____
(Type/Reason)   (Doctor Name)   (Date Cleared)

Date of Diagnosis: _____ Treatment: _____

_____
(Type/Reason)   (Doctor Name)   (Date Cleared)

MEDICAL IMPLANTS

_____
         (Type/Reason)   (Doctor Name)   (Date)

_____
    (Type/Reason)   *(Doctor Name)*   *(Date)*

_____
    (Type/Reason)   *(Doctor Name)*   *(Date)*

COSMETIC AND DENTAL IMPLANTS

_____
         (Type)   *(Doctor Name)*   *(Date)*

_____
         (Type)   *(Doctor Name)*   *(Date)*

SURGERY LIST

_____
(Type/Reason)   *(Doctor Name)*   *(Date)*   *(Special Instructions)*

_____
(Type/Reason)   *(Doctor Name)*   *(Date)*   *(Special Instructions)*

_____
(Type/Reason)   *(Doctor Name)*   *(Date)*   *(Special Instructions)*

_____
(Type/Reason)   *(Doctor Name)*   *(Date)*   *(Special Instructions)*

_____
(Type/Reason)   *(Doctor Name)*   *(Date)*   *(Special Instructions)*

FAMILY HISTORY

_____
(Diagnosis)   *(Name)*   *(Relationship)*

_____
(Diagnosis)   *(Name)*   *(Relationship)*

_____
(Diagnosis)   *(Name)*   *(Relationship)*

_____
(Diagnosis)   *(Name)*   *(Relationship)*

_____
(Diagnosis)   *(Name)*   *(Relationship)*

My Wishes upon Death

- ❖ **Breaking it All Down; Step by Step**

    - o **Photographs**

    - o **Death Certificate**

    - o **Details about Me**

        - ▪ **Obituary Information**

        - ▪ **Family**

    - o **My Wishes**

MY WISHES UPON DEATH

In this section we are going to talk about something most of us tend to avoid: **our own mortality**. It is not the easiest topic to think about, but if we take a step back and look at it with a practical lens, almost like handling an important life contract, we can take some of the emotional weight off and focus on clear communication. What a relief your loved one will have if they can go to one place and find everything they need.

Now, maybe planning all of this feels overwhelming, or maybe you have beliefs that say "Hey, once I'm gone, I'm gone—let the living handle it." And fair enough. But let me just say, that the people who must plan your funeral, memorial, burial, or Viking-style fireboat send-off, will be agonizing and carrying the weight of these decisions. I can tell you from experience, trying to plan a funeral, or decide arrangements without guidance is heartbreaking and stressful.

Even when someone talks casually about their preferences with loved ones, things can get messy. Imagine a group of people, each with a different version of what they remember you saying—trying to agree on what to do. Emotions are already high, and even the calmest family members can become overwhelmed, opinionated, or upset. It is nobody's fault; it is just what grief does sometimes.

The best way to avoid that kind of confusion is to write it down. Be clear. Be kind to your future self, and your family—by taking the time to organize your thoughts. We are going to go through it, step-by-step, and beginning to end. You are not alone in the process.

I feel confident saying that you will have lifted a heavy burden from the people you care about, and it is one of the kindest things you can do. And yes, you will likely feel a sense of relief when it is all down on paper.

BREAKING IT DOWN

Step #1 – PICTURES

The first thing on our list is easy. Go find your favorite picture of yourself. Now is not the time to be modest. People are going to spend endless hours digging through their computers, old photo albums, phones, and reaching out to others looking for what they believe to be a great picture of you. Why not pick the one you want? Are you a proud veteran? Do you have one that made you look like Marilyn Monroe or Marlon Brando that day? (Do not get hung up on the hot sexy 1950's references) My point is, do you want to be remembered from your younger years or current? We all have at minimum, one picture that we are most proud of. If you do not, get one taken. Regardless, find it, make sure it is printed, and affix it in the space provided in this book.

Your family will be asked for most likely twenty of their favorite pictures. If you have some that really bring you joy, get those put together in an envelope, label them, and keep in the book. *Whew! See that was not difficult! You just completed a huge step.*

Step #2 – DEATH CERTIFICATE

The second step is information that will be required for your death certificate. You are going to have one, you might as well fill out all the correct information. You might not have family, or if you do, not everyone might know these details. I was surprised to learn one of my siblings, whom was very close with my dad, did not know where my father was born. Being a genealogist, I have witnessed over and over wrong or missing information given by the informant. Save the informant responsible the anguish of getting it correct. *You are cruising through this!*

Step #3 – OBITUARY

In addition, there is another form that asks detailed questions about you. Why? Because, like it or not, you will most likely have an obituary. Someone will have to write it, and trust me, it is no easy task. Your family might be interviewed and asked to sum up your accomplishments, favorite pastimes, military background, and more. This is your chance to jot down the things you are most proud of, or what makes you, your unique self.

I chuckle as I write this because I can just picture my grandmother answering this question, and I know some of you will relate. Her response would have been**,** "I did not accomplish anything.

I just stayed home and raised my children." First, raising children is no small feat, it is an honorable and noteworthy accomplishment! But my grandmother's life was full of little details she may not have thought were important, yet to us, her descendants, they are treasures of information.

She maintained beautiful rose gardens, spent much of her life as a volunteer, and was the daughter of Sicilian immigrants who came through Ellis Island. Once I pressed her, I discovered that during WWII, she and her girlfriends worked at the Naval shipyard in Brooklyn, New York. She might have thought these were just ordinary parts of life, but to us, they are priceless pieces of our family history. Keep that in mind, you are special in more ways than you realize.

*This is **your** story—write it down. Whether you realize it or not, you have impacted the world, or at the very least, your community. Share it. Be proud of who you are and what you have seen or done. Most importantly, do not leave your loved ones scrambling to remember whether your favorite hobby was gardening or competitive bingo.*

Step #4 – CREMATED or BURIED

Okay, we got through some super easy steps, this next one might take some thought, but it needs to be decided, and written down. Do you want to be cremated or buried, and where? This is such a personal question and answer, and one that you might not be able to answer off the top of your head. I have included a pre-filled form in the next few pages which you can fill out with your choices and wishes. Do you want a traditional funeral? Do you have favorite music or scriptures? Do you want your ashes thrown into the wind off a boat? Do you want a funeral or maybe just a celebration of life? Once you pass, this will be a celebration of you. A celebration from the time you took your first beautiful breath, to your last, and all the time in-between.

I know many people view death and what comes after as nothing more than a burden to others. I am here to tell you; this is just simply not true! Let me share this scenario with you.

You pass and request a simple burial or cremation. You do not want anyone to fuss, or pay any attention to you. Meanwhile the people you have left behind struggle with what to do with their severe sadness, intense pain, or maybe even anger. They struggle with how to process their grief and abundance of emotions. The main purpose of a viewing and / or funeral is for people to honor you, and come together and support each other. They might stand around telling stories and talking about pictures they see. They could be laughing or crying, and probably both! It is part of processing grief and human emotions.

Something to think about—The ones you leave behind are left without you, and it does not matter how you departed whether sudden or a long-term disease. Denying your loved ones the opportunity to honor you could amplify their pain leaving them to suffer in solitude.

I understand this all too well, and I hope by sharing my story, it will give you more perspective and understanding. I remember my mother's viewing. She was young, and her passing very sudden. I really did not know a lot of details about her; she was just, Mom. We spent nearly every day on the phone together so I knew the basics, and subconsciously, like most people typically think, we have years and years of future to learn about Mom, as the individual woman.

As my siblings and I stood in the funeral parlor, in her honor, I was amazed by the number of people who came to pay their respects. Without the viewing, we never would have fully realized the impact she had beyond our own family. We met strangers who felt like friends, heard stories that made us laugh and cry, and discovered just how deeply she had touched the lives of others. To us, she was Mom, but to the world, she was Karen. That day, we glimpsed the beautiful legacy she quietly built, and in the midst of our grief, we found a comforting sense of connection and gratitude.

Once again, this is a personal choice, and no one can choose for you if you write down what you want. You can also pre-visit a funeral home and get all these details documented with them (Bring your book!). You may pay a deposit, but should not be required to. I do caution you in doing so, just in case they go out of business or change ownership. Make sure you get receipts, and have a clear outline of expectations. What is included, what is not. Ask questions about different scenarios of changed ownership etc. Do your due diligence and protect your funds.

Step #5 – HEADSTONE or URN

Choosing your headstone, color, and design might not be on your bucket list, but it is truly a gift to your loved ones. Without your input, they will be left guessing — and after a few tears and a lot of stress, guesswork can get a little... creative. One minute they are debating between "Elegant Gray" and "Sunset Rose," and the next thing you know, you are memorialized with a giant pink flamingo because someone thought it would "lighten the mood." Picking your style now saves everyone from a last-minute panic, or a possible family feud in a granite showroom, and ensures your final resting place actually feels more like *you*.

Believe it or not, you can now buy your headstone online! No, not from Amazon (yet), but there are plenty of companies ready to ship you the perfect piece of forever real-estate possibly at a much friendlier price than the "only game in town" monument dealer. The catch? Oh, there is always a catch. You must do a little homework. That means talking to the cemetery to get all the nitty-gritty required details: base size, thickness, installation rules, and how exactly you are getting this 400-pound beauty from "Point A to Plot B "— as well as installed plan. It is not quite as simple as free shipping and a promo code, but if you love saving money and do not mind asking questions, this could be a smart and satisfying alternative. Bonus points if you can say you scored a headstone deal *and* got cash back with your rewards card.

You can buy urns just about anywhere these days — online stores, Amazon, even Etsy if you want something that screams "artsy afterlife." Choices range from elegant marble to biodegradable tree pods to whatever Pinterest is pushing this week. Just make sure you check the size. You do not want to end up squeezed into something meant for a schnauzer. And while you are thinking about it, decide who gets to keep you. It is time to have these conversations, and write them down. Will you sit proudly on someone's fireplace? Travel from house to house like the family version of a Stanley Cup? Or maybe get planted under a tree so you can finally have a better backyard view than Uncle Bob? Making the call now saves your loved ones from a very weird game of rock, paper, scissors later.

This page is where you are going to place your favorite picture (s) of yourself

Death Certificate Information

Your Full Name: _____
                        First   *Middle*   *Last*   *Maiden*

Your DOB: _____ Place of Birth _____
                                                          (City and State)

Home Address: _____

Education and Occupational Degrees Held: _____

Employer: _____ Business/Industry: _____

Next of Kin: _____ Relationship: _____

Next of Kin Address: _____

Religious Affiliation: _____ Place of Worship: _____

Father's Full Name: _____ Father's Birthplace: _____

Mother's Full Name: _____ Mother's Birthplace: _____

Married?   Yes   or   No

Spouse Full Name: _____

Date of Marriage: _____ Location: _____

Previous Marriage: Name _____

Date: _____ Date Dissolved: _____

Military/Veteran information with Branch of Service: _____

War time Service: yes or no   Serial Number: _____

DETAILS ABOUT ME
(Information that might be included in your Obituary)

My full Name: _____

Where did you grow up? _____

What high school did you go to? Where? When? _____

Belong to any clubs or sports? _____

What do you remember most about your childhood? _____

_____

Did you attend College? Which one? Where? When? _____

Belong to any clubs or sports? _____

What did you major in? _____

Did you get another type of education or learn the trades? _____

What was your first job? Age? _____

Where did you work the longest? _____

List any Clubs and/or organizations? _____

_____

Any awards or accomplishments? _____

What do you want to be known for? _____

Name a few hobbies you have enjoyed throughout your life? _____

What are your current hobbies? _____

Have you ever volunteered? _____

What are somethings you are most proud of? _____

_____

Military Service? _____ Branch? _____

Rank? _____ Any awards or ribbons? _____

What was your dates of service? _____ Why did you choose to go into the military?

_____

Have you traveled? _____ Where? _____

What is your favorite activity? _____

Do you attend church or any place of worship? _____

Spouse: *(Include maiden name if applicable)*

_____
(Social Security No.)   *(Name)*   *(Phone)*   *(Address)*

Previous Spouse (s): *(Include maiden name if applicable)*

_____
(Name)   *(Phone)*   *(Address)*   *(Divorce Date)*

_____
(Name)   *(Phone)*   *(Address)*   *(Divorce Date)*

Children:

_____
(Relationship)   *(Name)*   *(Phone)*   *(Address)*

_____
(Relationship)   *(Name)*   *(Phone)*   *(Address)*

_____
(Relationship)   *(Name)*   *(Phone)*   *(Address)*

_____
(Relationship)   *(Name)*   *(Phone)*   *(Address)*

_____
(Relationship)   *(Name)*   *(Phone)*   *(Address)*

_____
(Relationship)   *(Name)*   *(Phone)*   *(Address)*

Siblings:

_____
(Relationship)   (Name)   (Phone)   (Address)

_____
(Relationship)   (Name)   (Phone)   (Address)

_____
(Relationship)   (Name)   (Phone)   (Address)

_____
(Relationship)   (Name)   (Phone)   (Address)

_____
(Relationship)   (Name)   (Phone)   (Address)

_____
(Relationship)   (Name)   (Phone)   (Address)

Grandchildren:

_____
(Relationship)   (Name)   (Phone)   (Address)

_____
(Relationship)   (Name)   (Phone)   (Address)

_____
(Relationship)   (Name)   (Phone)   (Address)

_____
(Relationship)   (Name)   (Phone)   (Address)

_____
(Relationship)   (Name)   (Phone)   (Address)

_____
(Relationship)   (Name)   (Phone)   (Address)

_____
(Relationship)   (Name)   (Phone)   (Address)

_____
(Relationship)   (Name)   (Phone)   (Address)

_____
(Relationship)   (Name)   (Phone)   (Address)

Great Grandchildren:

| (Relationship) | (Name) | (Phone) | (Address) |

| (Relationship) | (Name) | (Phone) | (Address) |

| (Relationship) | (Name) | (Phone) | (Address) |

| (Relationship) | (Name) | (Phone) | (Address) |

| (Relationship) | (Name) | (Phone) | (Address) |

| (Relationship) | (Name) | (Phone) | (Address) |

| (Relationship) | (Name) | (Phone) | (Address) |

| (Relationship) | (Name) | (Phone) | (Address) |

| (Relationship) | (Name) | (Phone) | (Address) |

| (Relationship) | (Name) | (Phone) | (Address) |

| (Relationship) | (Name) | (Phone) | (Address) |

| (Relationship) | (Name) | (Phone) | (Address) |

Do you have additional family members or close friends that need to be reached?

| (Relationship) | (Name) | (Phone) | (Address) |

| (Relationship) | (Name) | (Phone) | (Address) |

_____
(Relationship)   (Name)   (Phone)   (Address)

_____
(Relationship)   (Name)   (Phone)   (Address)

_____
(Relationship)   (Name)   (Phone)   (Address)

_____
(Relationship)   (Name)   (Phone)   (Address)

Who played an important role in your life? _____
_____
_____
_____

If there is anything else or is there a story you feel important to share, write it down here:
_____
_____
_____
_____
_____
_____
_____

Do you have any regrets?
_____
_____
_____
_____

There is a place to write messages to your loved ones in the back of this book

All about Me

- **Cheese or No Cheese**

- **My Taste Buds**

  - What I Like and What I Do Not

- **My Comfort**

  - What Makes Me Comfortable

- **My Entertainment**

  - What Things I Enjoy

- **My Personality**

  - What Brings Me Joy

- **Everything Else**

  - A Place You Can Add Your Own

ALL ABOUT ME

CHEESE OR NO CHEESE

Cheese or no cheese is a part of this workbook that is so important and critical to fill out. Life-or-death? Maybe not. But do you really trust your loved ones to know your favorite foods? Let's be honest—how many loved ones forget anniversaries or birthdays, or gift you something so off-base that you wonder if they picked it out in the dark? I am not here to call anyone out (okay, maybe just a little), but if you suddenly could not communicate, would your family know your absolute disgust for Curry spice? Or that you would choose chocolate over vanilla every time? Do not leave your culinary fate in the hands of guesswork—fill this out and save yourself from a lifetime of unwanted nuts in your cookies.

This section is near and dear to me because it taught me things about my dad I never would have known. My dad was the kind of man who never complained. If you made him something unappetizing, he would just eat it, no fuss. But every now and then, if you paid close attention, you would catch the face—a tiny grimace, a slight hesitation. That is when I knew I had committed a culinary crime.

Take strawberries, for example. I constantly brought him fresh fruit, and he happily ate it… except for berries. Almost annoyed, I finally asked him, "Dad, why are you not eating the strawberries?" His response? "I never liked them." "Why?" I chuckled. "The seeds get stuck in my teeth." I remember rolling my eyes, well okay then, no more fresh berries for you!

Then, there is the famous cheeseburger saga. My dad loved to grill, and burgers were always on the menu. Despite raising me, feeding me, and loving me for decades, the man could never remember that I did not like cheese on my burger. Every single family gathering, without fail, he would yell out, "I know one of you doesn't like cheese—who is it?" And with a dramatic eye roll, I would reply, "It's me, Dad." Every. Single. Time. Some things just never stuck.

I share these stories not because my dad did not love me (he did, endlessly) or because he did not care (he absolutely did), but because sometimes, our brains just do not retain the details. So, my friends, do yourself a favor, fill out this section. Save your loved ones the guesswork and yourself from a lifetime of unwanted cheese.

"MES PAPILLES PARFAITES" – MY TASTE BUDS HAVE IMPECCABLE TASTE!

My food Allergies: _____

I am a Vegetarian _____ Vegan _____ Lactose Intolerant _____

I need a diabetic menu _____ Gluten-Free _____ I eat everything _____

If I could ban certain foods from existence, what would they be? _____
_____

Foods I love _____
_____

I crave, Salty or Sweet _____

Favorite Salty go to: _____ Favorite sweet go to: _____

Cheese or no cheese on my burger? _____ Cooked? Rare   Medium   Burnt

Vegetable I do not like? _____ Favorites _____

Favorite Soups: _____ Type of Salads: _____

I like my eggs? Hard boiled ___ Scrambled ___ Runny ___ Over light ___ Hate Eggs ___

Bacon or Sausage: _____ Crispy or Not: _____ Home fries: Crispy or Not: _____

Favorite Sandwiches: _____

Favorite Snacks: _____

Favorite desserts: _____

Favorite Flavors Ice cream: _____

Favorite drink? Carbonation or not? _____

I like Coffee and/or Tea _____ I like it with _____

If I could only eat one type of cuisine for the rest of my life, it be? _____

MY COMFORT

My comfortable indoor temperature is _____ I do like it cooler to sleep? _____

I fall asleep easier -- Any special routine? Quiet or back ground noise? _____

I like my environment quiet and organized, or energized (music, TV, conversation) _____

This helps me feel safe and secure _____

This makes me feel anxious _____

I like alone time or having visitors _____

Fabrics I love or dislike _____

Scents or smells that soothe me? (Lavender, vanilla etc.) _____

Gives me strength when feeling uncertain _____

I have touch sensitivities? (Gentle touch only, avoid certain areas, etc.) _____

MY ENTERTAINMENT

I love my couch or recliner _____ Favorite blanket / pillow _____

Favorite Movies and Genre: _____

I do/don't like to keep up with Current News and Events? _____

Favorite TV Shows? Genre: _____

Favorite Way to spend down time: Reading-Genre _____ Author _____

Painting _____ Gardening _____ Tinkering _____ Cooking _____ Puzzles _____

Hanging with friends/family _____ Watching Sports _____ Other: _____

_____

Music preference and Artists: _____

I enjoy to get out and explore Nature _____ Museums _____ Fishing _____

Favorite season _____ Why? _____

Favorite holiday _____

Traditions I hope to continue? _____

_____

_____

_____

MY PERSONALITY

What makes me laugh the most? _____

I like to lounge in the morning, wake up slowly _____ Get up early and get my day started _____

I like to stay up late _____ Get to bed early _____

The types of people I like to be around? Comedians _____ Techies _____ Serious _____

Spiritual ____ Quiet _____ Life of the party _____ Other _____

The kinds of personalities I pray I will not be stranded on an island with? _____

_____

I like to be clean shaven / hair and make-up done every day _____ Hair brushed is fine _____

I prefer to look my very best _____ Business casual _____ Comfy sweats _____

If I have company coming, I prefer _____

These things hurt my feelings _____

This completely ticks me off _____

Attributes I value in others around me _____

EVERYTHING ELSE

_____

_____

My Final Wishes

- ❖ **Burial Instructions**
  - o **Details and Location**
- ❖ **Cremation Instructions**
  - o **Ashes**
- ❖ **Service Instructions**
  - o **Music**
  - o **Readings**
- ❖ **Organ and / or Body Donation**

MY FINAL WISHES

Planning in advance for your funeral, and communicating your wishes accomplishes several objectives. Sure, the obvious reason ensures things go the way you would like them to go, but equally important, it may alleviate potential family disputes. Grief and pain of losing a loved one can spark different emotions and reactions in different people. Sometimes knowing exactly what your loved one wanted eases this pain and anxiety.

If you are able, having things paid for in advance will also reduce any burden to those making your arrangements.

- You can purchase insurance from a reputable insurance company, but make sure you document on the insurance page the name of the company, and where the documents are.
- You can create a savings account and designate someone you trust to use the funds for your burial or cremation
- You may want to avoid funeral or cremation companies directly as they may go out of business or refuse to cover certain things if you move away. Company policies could change without you knowing
- Burial Insurance is similar to term Life insurance, whereas it has no cash value

If you choose cremation and have ideas of what you would like your loved ones to do with your ashes there are some things you should consider when sharing your wishes:

- Pay attention to your state and local laws when scattering ashes in oceans, forests, or public spaces
- If you want to have your ashes at sea, you must obtain a permit from the Environmental Protection Agency and place ashes no closer than three nautical miles from the shoreline.
- State parks often require permits

If you would like donations to be made in your honor, make sure you share your favorite organization. It might be nice to include your reasons as to why you chose this organization

_____

_____

FULL NAME: _____ **DATE** _____

When I pass, I choose to be: Buried _____   Cremated _____

Would you like to have your body and/or Organs donated?   Yes ____   No _____

BURIAL INSTRUCTIONS

Funeral Home Preference: _____
                                     (Name)   *(Phone)*   *(Email Address)*

I have a Prepaid Funeral Home Contract With_____

My Cemetery Preference: _____
                              (Cemetery Name/Location)   *(Phone)*

I have a **Prepaid** Burial Plot Located at: _____
                                        (Cemetery)   *(Lot No.)*

I have Burial Insurance Yes _____   No _____   (If yes see Insurance Page)

I am allowed to have Free Military Burial: Yes ____   No ____   Military ID No._____

Preferred Type of Casket: _____

I would like to have a certain type, style, and color of headstone: _____
_____

I have a Prepaid stone with: _____

I would like to be wearing the following clothes/outfit: _____
_____

Pallbearer Preference and Contact Information:

1._____
     (Name)   *(Phone)*   *(Email Address)*

2._____
     (Name)   *(Phone)*   *(Email Address)*

3._____
     (Name)   *(Phone)*   *(Email Address)*

4._____
     (Name)   *(Phone)*   *(Email Address)*

5. _____
       (Name)   *(Phone)*   *(Email Address)*

6. _____
       (Name)   *(Phone)*   *(Email Address)*

CREMATION INSTRUCTIONS

Type of Urn for my ashes: _____

Location of pre-purchased Urn: _____

Prepaid Cremation arrangements: _____

Location of Contract: _____

I would like to be wearing the following clothes/outfit: _____

_____

Where should my ashes be put? Or held with whom?

_____

_____

MY SERVICE INSTRUCTIONS

I would like a: Church Service _____   Funeral Home Service _____   No Service _____

If no service is checked, would you prefer to have a Celebration of Life?   Yes _____   No _____

If yes, Where? _____

Name and location of church and/or funeral home or Service Location:

_____   _____

I would like to have the following Music at my service:

     1. _____

     2. _____

     3. _____

I would like to have the following poems, scripture, and/or readings: (List who you would like to read them if you have a preference)

1. _____
2. _____
3. _____
4. _____

Flower Preferences: Do you have a favorite Color or type of flower? _____

_____

Additional Information or request for your service: _____

_____

Friends and people that have been special to me that my next of kin may not know how to reach:

(Name)	(Address)	(Phone)	(Email)
(Name)	(Address)	(Phone)	(Email)
(Name)	(Address)	(Phone)	(Email)
(Name)	(Address)	(Phone)	(Email)
(Name)	(Address)	(Phone)	(Email)

ORGAN AND/OR BODY DONATION

| (Name of Organization) | (Address) | (Phone) |

Location of documents with authorization: _____

Instructions: _____

_____

Dependents and Pets

- ❖ **Types of Dependents**

- ❖ **Dependents – All Minor Children**
  - Adopted and Foster Children
  - Insurance
  - Location of Legal Information

- ❖ **Dependents – Parents or Others**
  - Type and Contact List

- ❖ **Pets**
  - A List of all Pets
  - Care Guide and Instructions
  - Name of New Guardian
  - Medical Information

DEPENDENTS AND PETS

DEPENDENT TYPES

When we think of dependents our minds automatically think of our minor children. However, there are several additional types of dependents you may not have thought about. Naturally you are legally responsible for your minor or disabled children, and you will need a legal will or trust documenting their new guardian. Just a reminder that verbally telling someone is not legally binding, and your wishes may not come to fruition if it is not done with legal signed documents.

It could take some thought and planning regarding any minor or disabled children. When choosing a new legal guardian be mindful about where they attend school, and will they have to move. Will their new guardian be capable to handle their emotional and financial needs? Do they follow your values? Think about their long-term health and well-being as well as their financial stability when choosing their new guardian. I suggest including a contingency plan in your legal documents because situations can change.

The selected guardian does not have to be the person managing their assets. You have the right to name a different guardian for their inherited assets. The following section is where you can put your details. Important additional information that would not be included in a long estate document.

There are other additional types of dependents you might be responsible for such as an elderly parent, and do not forget your pets! If you pass or become incapacitated, you need to have a plan for them too. No one loves them as much as we do, and no one knows their needs like we do. It needs to be written down and discussed with the person you allocate. Especially with pets. Make sure that this person is willing to take on the responsibility.

DEPENDENTS

1. _____
    (Name)　　　　　　　*(DOB)*　　　　　*(Place of Birth)*　　　*(Location of Birth Certificate)*

_____
    (Primary Health Provider)　　　　　*(Address)*　　　　*(Phone)*　　　*(Email)*

_____
    (Health Insurance)　　*(Ins. ID No.)*　　　*(Guardian)*　　　*(Financial Guardian)*

2. _____
    (Name)　　　　　　　*(DOB)*　　　　　*(Place of Birth)*　　　*(Location of Birth Certificate)*

_____
    (Primary Health Provider)　　　　　*(Address)*　　　　*(Phone)*　　　*(Email)*

_____
    (Health Insurance)　　*(Ins. ID No.)*　　　*(Guardian)*　　　*(Financial Guardian)*

3. _____
    (Name)　　　　　　　*(DOB)*　　　　　*(Place of Birth)*　　　*(Location of Birth Certificate)*

_____
    (Primary Health Provider)　　　　　*(Address)*　　　　*(Phone)*　　　*(Email)*

_____
    (Health Insurance)　　*(Ins. ID No.)*　　　*(Guardian)*　　　*(Financial Guardian)*

4. _____
    (Name)　　　　　　　*(DOB)*　　　　　*(Place of Birth)*　　　*(Location of Birth Certificate)*

_____
    (Primary Health Provider)　　　　　*(Address)*　　　　*(Phone)*　　　*(Email)*

_____
    (Health Insurance)　　*(Ins. ID No.)*　　　*(Guardian)*　　　*(Financial Guardian)*

Additional Information (Include Social Security Numbers and Schools or facilities):

_____

_____

_____

ADDITIONAL DEPENDENTS

1. _____
   (Name of Person)   (Relationship)   (DOB)

   _____
   (Address)   (Phone)   (Emergency Contact)

   _____
   (Type of Assistance provided)

2. _____
   (Name of Person)   (Relationship)   (DOB)

   _____
   (Address)   (Phone)   (Emergency Contact)

   _____
   (Type of Assistance provided)

3. _____
   (Name of Person)   (Relationship)   (DOB)

   _____
   (Address)   (Phone)   (Emergency Contact)

   _____
   (Type of Assistance provided)

Additional Information: _____

_____

_____

PETS

1. _____
   (Name of Pet)   (Breed)   (DOB)   (License & Chip Information)

   _____
   (Veterinarian)   (Address)   (Phone)

   _____
   (Brand of Food)   (Quantity and Frequency)   (Allergies)

   _____
   (Pet Insurance)   (Policy No.)   (Contact)

(Medications)	(Reason)	(Frequency)
(Medications)	(Reason)	(Frequency)
(Medications)	(Reason)	(Frequency)
(New Custodian)	(Phone)	(Address)

Care Instructions: _____

_____

_____

_____

2. _____

(Name of Pet)	(Breed)	(DOB)	(License & Chip Information)
(Veterinarian)	(Address)		(Phone)
(Brand of Food)	(Quantity and Frequency)		(Allergies)
(Pet Insurance)	(Policy No.)		(Contact)
(Medications)	(Reason)		(Frequency)
(Medications)	(Reason)		(Frequency)
(Medications)	(Reason)		(Frequency)
(New Custodian)	(Phone)		(Address)

Care Instructions: _____

_____

_____

_____

Insurances

- ❖ **Medical Health**
- ❖ **Dental**
- ❖ **Vision**
- ❖ **Long Term Care**
- ❖ **Burial**
- ❖ **Accidental Death & Dismemberment**
- ❖ **Life**
- ❖ **Home and Property**
- ❖ **Liability**
- ❖ **Umbrella**
- ❖ **Additional Asset**
- ❖ **Auto**
- ❖ **Equipment**
  - o **Offroad**
  - o **Trailers**
  - o **Yard Equipment**

INSURANCES

We all have many types of insurance — health, life, car, home, pet, phone, etc. This section will help you create one central spot to document and keep track of everything you have. Let us be honest; it is hard enough for us to remember our own policies, due dates, and contact information. Now imagine someone else trying to piece it all together like a scavenger hunt... without a map... under extreme emotional stress. A little organization now, can save your loved ones from needing a detective badge later.

Let's go through them together, and if you have additional insurance that I did not add, there will be a place at the end where you can include it.

MEDICAL HEALTH INSURANCE

*Primary Carrier: _____ Member ID: _____

Subscriber Name: _____ Company: _____

Contact No. _____ URL: _____

*Secondary Carrier: _____ Member ID: _____

Subscriber Name: _____ Company: _____

Contact No. _____ URL: _____

*Pharmaceutical Ins. Carrier: _____ Member ID: _____

Location of Pharmacy or Mail in Address: _____

_____

DENTAL

Agency: _____ Policy No. _____

Contact: Name / Address / Phone_____

VISION

Agency: _____ Policy No. _____

Contact: Name / Address / Phone _____

LONG - TERM CARE

Carrier: _____ Member ID: _____

Subscriber Name: _____ Company/Agency: _____

Contact No. _____ URL: _____

BURIAL

Agency: _____ Policy No. _____

Contact: Name / Address / Phone _____

Date Initiated _____ Amount: $_____

ACCIDENTAL DEATH and DISMEMBERMENT

Company/Agency: _____ Policy No: _____

Contact No. _____ URL: _____

LIFE

1. Agency: _____ Policy No. _____

Contact: Name / Address / Phone _____

Term _____ or Whole Life _____ Period _____

Amount: $_____

Beneficiary: _____ % _____ Relationship: _____

Beneficiary: _____ % _____ Relationship: _____

Beneficiary: _____ % _____ Relationship: _____

Beneficiary: _____ % _____ Relationship: _____

2. Agency: _____ Policy No. _____

Contact: Name / Address / Phone_____

Term _____ or Whole Life _____ Period _____

Amount: $_____

Beneficiary: _____ % _____ Relationship: _____

Beneficiary: _____ % _____ Relationship: _____

Beneficiary: _____ % _____ Relationship: _____

Beneficiary: _____ % _____ Relationship: _____

3. Agency: _____ Policy No. _____

Contact: Name / Address / Phone_____

Term _____ or Whole Life _____ Period _____

Amount: $_____

Beneficiary: _____ % _____ Relationship: _____

Beneficiary: _____ % _____ Relationship: _____

Beneficiary: _____ % _____ Relationship: _____

Beneficiary: _____ % _____ Relationship: _____

HOME INSURANCE TYPES

HOMEOWNERS / PROPERTY (This could also include Renters Insurance)

Address No. 1

Company/Agency: _____ Policy No.: _____

Address of Property: _____

Contact No. _____ URL: _____

Address No. 2

Company/Agency: _____ Policy No.: _____

Address of Property: _____

Contact No. _____ URL: _____

LIABILITY

Company/Agency: _____ Policy No.: _____

Contact No. _____ URL: _____

UMBRELLA

Company/Agency: _____ Policy No.: _____

Contact No. _____ URL: _____

ADDITIONAL ASSET

Company/Agency: _____ Policy No.: _____

Contact No. _____ URL: _____

AUTO INSURANCE

Vehicle No. 1

Company/Agency: _____ Policy No.: _____

Make / Model / Year: _____

Contact No. _____ URL: _____

Vehicle No. 2

Company/Agency: _____ Policy No.: _____

Make / Model / Year: _____

Contact No. _____ URL: _____

Vehicle No. 3

Company/Agency: _____ Policy No.: _____

Make / Model / Year: _____

Contact No. _____ URL: _____

Vehicle No. 4

Company/Agency: _____ Policy No.: _____

Make / Model / Year: _____

Contact No. _____ URL: _____

PET INSURANCE

Pets Name: _____

Company/Agency: _____ Policy No.: _____

Contact No. _____ URL: _____

EQUIPMENT INSURANCE (This could be Trailers, Off Road Vehicles, or Yard Equip.)

TYPE: _____

Company/Agency: _____ Policy No.: _____

Make / Model / Year: _____

Contact No. _____ URL: _____

TYPE: _____

Company/Agency: _____ Policy No.: _____

Make / Model / Year: _____

Contact No. _____ URL: _____

TYPE: _____

Company/Agency: _____ Policy No.: _____

Make / Model / Year: _____

Contact No. _____ URL: _____

TYPE: _____

Company/Agency: _____ Policy No.: _____

Make / Model / Year: _____

Contact No. _____ URL: _____

Property and Assets

- ❖ **Homes and Your Heirs**
- ❖ **Digital Activity**
    - o **All Your Devices**
    - o **Social Media**
    - o **Email Accounts**
    - o **Website Accounts**
    - o **Internet Security**
- ❖ **Real Estate and Rentals**
    - o **All Your Stuff**
    - o **Property Tax Tip**
- ❖ **Properties**
    - o **Real Estate**
        - ▪ **Everything Related to the Home**
    - o **Safety Deposit Box**
    - o **Storage Units**
- ❖ **All the Little Things**

PROPERTY & ASSETS

DID YOU KNOW?

Inheriting a home with a Mortgage? Sometimes that mortgage has a very low interest rate and you might want to just assume the mortgage without refinancing or establishing a new loan. In 1982, a federal law established the Garn-St. Germain Act. This overrides State law and allows certain heirs (such as spouse and children) to inherit a home and continue to pay its existing mortgage without refinancing. Most of the time a FHA and VA loans can be transferred, while others may not. It is always good to know your lenders policies.

The 5-Year Look-Back Rule: Retroactive Finance

Imagine Uncle Sam as a nosy neighbor with binoculars and a calendar, peeking over your financial fence. The moment you apply for Medicaid to help pay for long-term care, he says, "Hold up! Let's rewind five years and see what kind of shenanigans you have been up to."

That is right — the **5-Year Look-Back** is Uncle Sam's version of a financial flashback episode. He is not judging your taste in wallpaper or the time you bought a jet ski "for the grandkids" — he just wants to know if you have **given away money or assets** to dodge paying for care. Spoiler alert: If you have, he is not thrilled.

Transferred your lake house to Cousin Eddie for a dollar? Donated your vintage Beanie Baby collection (worth millions, of course) to your cat's trust fund? Uncle Sam sees that as a foul play — and he is ready to throw a flag and **penalize** you with a delay in benefits.

So, moral of the story: If you are planning to apply for Medicaid, do not try to play financial hide-and-seek in the last five years. Uncle Sam's look-back game is strong, and he has got receipts. Seek a Legal financial Planner and / or Elder Attorney when planning out your future.

Prep Your Home

You spend so much of your time updating your home for your future. You would be surprised of how much you do. Each house is different, and has its unique character and idiosyncrasies. You know all those things, but if someone else was to walk in, and take over, it could be very frustrating!

This is a great time to document valuables within your home that might have maintenance and instructions. Get this information put together and document where they are. You buy a new refrigerator or washer / dryer, add it to the folder. If your property has insect or rodent problems and you hire an exterminator, write it down! There is nothing worse than your children or your caregiver starting from scratch. You have done it, and maybe had experience with someone you have used for years. These companies will be more than accommodating assisting the person helping you when you cannot handle it yourself. Below is a central place to put all this information.

***TIP** — My dad made paint sticks of every paint color for each room. It was dipped in the color paint, and labeled with the brand, type and size of paint, and the formula. Brands will change the formulas over time, putting the formula is important. He then drilled a hole in the bottom of the paint sticks and used a repurposed old bread zip tie to keep them all together. This was brilliant!*

DIGITAL ACTIVITY

PASSWORD SECURITY

We live in a very scary world, full of scammers and digital con artists. Here is my suggestion: Create different passwords for each account. Yes, every single one. Many companies already require you to change your passwords regularly anyway. My suggestion is to write the information on a sticky and put over this section. They may change frequently, and you can toss the sticky when things change verses putting it permanently in the book. For security's sake, remember to create passwords that are unique for each, and every account.

Now… how do you create a password? You want something memorable, right? But the more memorable it is to you, the more obvious it might be to someone trying to break in and steal everything you have. Let's rewind for a moment to the pre-internet days. Back then, passwords were easy. You were asked for one, and you proudly came up with *your* special word. That word was yours and yours alone, and you used it for everything. DONE!

Then came the internet and all your financial institutions wanted you to log in, and they required you to use a capital letter. No problem we thought to ourselves —we just capitalized the first letter of our very special word. DONE!

Suddenly, a new rule was required: ***Add a number***. Fine. We all sighed, sat back, and added the first number we could think of — Number **1**. DONE!

Feeling clever and safe, we logged into our top-secret financial accounts like digital spies. Capital letter? ☑ Number? ☑ We were basically becoming cybersecurity experts.

But wait—***big bold red letters*** popped up screaming: "You are not secure enough! Please add a special character."

A **what now?** Special character? After a mild existential crisis, we scanned the list of options we were given to choose from and found a familiar face: the Exclamation point. Perfect! A little dramatic flair. DONE!!!

We felt invincible. But now, as you are reading this, ask yourself: **how many accounts still use some version of that same "very special" password with a No.1 and Exclamation!**

If the answer is more than one—**CHANGE YOUR PASSWORDS**.

Seriously. Internet crime is on the rise, and if you reuse passwords, it only takes one breach to wipe out everything. This book can help you keep track of them all.

INTERNET SECURITY

I **cannot** emphasize enough how important it is to stay vigilant on the internet. I know, I know—I sound like my grandparents when I say, ***"What is this world coming to?!"*** But honestly, have you seen the internet lately? If my grandparents were around today, they would probably throw their flip phones at the wall and go live off the grid. And honestly? Not a bad plan.

Everywhere you turn, there's fraud, scams, shady deals, and someone trying to trick you out of your hard-earned money. It could be as simple as your cable company (who somehow *always* finds a way to charge you more each month), or an email claiming you have won a $100 gift card… if you just "confirm your identity" by typing in your Social Security number and the name of your childhood pet.

Let me tell you—these scammers, they are professionals**.** They could win Oscars for how convincing they are. If this has ever happened to you, do *not* beat yourself up. You are not alone. I have been scammed myself, multiple times. From mystery charges on my credit card to packages that never arrived (but hey, at least the website looked fancy…).

Just recently, I heard a story that truly broke my heart. An elderly woman, recently widowed, received an email claiming her late husband owed back taxes. Out of duty, she called the number. The "company" (and I use that term very loosely) set up recurring payments. They took just enough each month to fly under the radar, and by the time her children figured it out, she had paid **over seventy thousand dollars**. The scammers were overseas. The money? Gone.

So yeah, the internet can be like a dark alley in a bad action movie. But do not panic! You do not need to become a hacker or go live in the woods. You just need to arm yourself with knowledge and a healthy dose of skepticism. Personally, I live by the motto: **Trust, but verify.**

HOW TO PROTECT YOURSELF ONLINE

The internet can be a tricky place—but with a few smart habits, you can stay one step ahead of scammers and fraudsters. Here is a handy guide to help you stay safe:

🔒 **Passwords & Authentication**

- **Change your passwords regularly** and use different ones for each account. (Yes, I said it before. I am saying it again. It is that important!) Use strong, unique passwords for each account.
- **Enable two-factor authentication** (2FA) wherever it is available. It adds an extra layer of protection; like a secret handshake for your accounts.

📧 Email Tips

- **Create two email accounts**:
  - One for personal use: banking, bills, and close communication.
  - One for shopping and general online activity. You will notice this second inbox fills up with spam and scam attempts faster than you can say "unsubscribe."
- **Use initials instead of your full name** when signing up for services you do not fully trust. If scam emails start using that variation, you will know where they came from.

Reminder: The IRS will never contact you by email, phone, or with colorful, cheerful mail. If it looks too flashy, it is probably a scam. If they want you, it is going to be boring, scary, and very official-looking.

⚠ Spotting & Avoiding Scams

- **Never click on suspicious links** or open unexpected attachments. even if it looks like it came from Aunt Karen. Especially if it says "Check this out 😜."
- **Always double-check email addresses** and website URLs. If something seems off (like amazon.com with a weird "a"), it probably is.
- **If it sounds too good to be true**—it probably involves losing money and gaining regret.
- **Trust but verify**:
  - Got an email saying your subscription is expiring or your account needs updating? Do not click it. Visit the website directly and check your account.

🧹 Digital Housekeeping

- **Delete old accounts** you no longer use. Less exposure, fewer risks.
- **Install antivirus and anti-malware** software on all your devices. It is like sunscreen for your devices—protects you even when you do not notice it.

📱 Mobile Device Safety

- **Lock devices** using a password, PIN, or biometric login (like fingerprint or face ID).
- **Turn off Bluetooth and location services** when you are not using them. No need to broadcast your every move.
- **Enable remote wipe** on your phone in case it is lost or stolen— just in case it ever ends up in the hands of someone who does not deserve your vacation photos or banking app.

By following these steps, you are not just protecting your devices—you are protecting your peace of mind. The goal is not to be paranoid; it is to be prepared. Stay sharp out there!

DIGITAL DEVICES & LOG IN

Wifi: Login: _____ Password: _____

Wifi: Login: _____ Password: _____

Wifi: Login: _____ Password: _____

Phone/Voicemail: _____ Password: _____

Phone/Voicemail: _____ Password: _____

Computer: _____ Password: _____

Computer: _____ Password: _____

Computer: _____ Password: _____

Laptop: _____ Password: _____

Laptop: _____ Password: _____

Tablet: _____ Password: _____

Other: _____ Password: _____

Other: _____ Password: _____

Other: _____ Password: _____

Other: _____ Password: _____

SOCIAL MEDIA

_____ _____ _____ _____
(Platform)   *(ID)*   *(Password)* *(EMAIL ASSOCIATED)*

_____ _____ _____ _____
(Platform)   *(ID)*   *(Password)* *(EMAIL ASSOCIATED)*

_____ _____ _____ _____
(Platform)   *(ID)*   *(Password)* *(EMAIL ASSOCIATED)*

_____ _____ _____ _____
(Platform)   *(ID)*   *(Password)* *(EMAIL ASSOCIATED)*

_____ _____ _____ _____
(Platform)   *(ID)*   *(Password)* *(EMAIL ASSOCIATED)*

EMAIL ACCOUNTS

_____ _____ _____ _____
(Carrier)   *(ID)*   *(Password)* *(EMAIL ADDRESS)*

_____ _____ _____ _____
(Carrier)   *(ID)*   *(Password)* *(EMAIL ADDRESS)*

_____ _____ _____ _____
(Carrier)   *(ID)*   *(Password)* *(EMAIL ADDRESS)*

_____ _____ _____ _____
(Carrier)   *(ID)*   *(Password)* *(EMAIL ADDRESS)*

_____ _____ _____ _____
(Carrier)   *(ID)*   *(Password)* *(EMAIL ADDRESS)*

WEBSITE ACCOUNTS

_____ _____ _____ _____
(Website Address)   *(ID)*   *(Password)* *(EMAIL ASSOCIATED)*

(Website Address)	(ID)	(Password)	(EMAIL ASSOCIATED
(Website Address)	*(ID)*	*(Password)*	*(EMAIL ASSOCIATED*

REAL-ESTATE AND/OR RENTALS

OUR TREASURES

Whether you own a home, or live in a rental, or own multiple properties, you have stuff! Stuff here, stuff there, stuff in closets, stuff underbeds, in corners, garages, and sheds! Some even pay for storage units to hold their stuff!

We spend our whole lives collecting stuff that for whatever reason we think we need, or makes our lives easier, or sometimes it is just because it sparkles! No one more guilty than myself! As we age, and start thinking about our mortality, we think about who we would like to pass on that special heirloom to, or who would want our special stuff.

To us, the owner, some of our items of stuff is just priceless! For me, it is the heirlooms from my ancestors. For others, it is just the treasures that they have collected, and yet for others it could be something completely different. If you have children, grandchildren, or someone really close to you that you want to leave your stuff to, it is time to evaluate (*and maybe even thin out*)!

HAVE A CONVERSATION

First, it is time to have an honest conversation with your loved ones about what they actually want — and what they would secretly rather not inherit. You might have something that is incredibly special to you, but if nobody knows its story, it could end up in a donation bin faster than you can say "estate sale." Take me, for example: I have a few of my mother's treasures that I know my son would glance at, shrug, and toss without a second thought. Not because he did not love his grandmother, but because to him, it is just "some old thing." Meanwhile, his daughters, my granddaughters, might think it is the coolest thing ever, simply because it once belonged to their great-grandmother. The point is, if you do not tell them, they will not know. And if they do not know, they will probably toss it... right next to the lava lamp and the mystery keys.

WHY WAIT

In my experience, it is helpful to make the offer to the people you love to come point out what is meaningful to them. You can share the stories about the item; that alone makes it mean something more than the actual object alone. If it is something you no longer need, give it to them!! You need to thin your stuff! What a joy to see on their faces while you are alive, rather than an item that gets handed down from a will, or could get tossed in a dumpster.

To me, having my special things landing in a dumpster is horrifying! My grandchildren are currently too young to give anything yet. You might be in that situation, or you might not be quite ready to let go of your special item. My advice, put a tag under the item. What it is, any known monetary value, and who you think should have it. Label it!

In this section, I have created a place you can document items that are special to you. Either way, it is time to thin your stuff. Simplify your life. We all get to a place when we cannot move as much, or clean as well. Having an organized simple space does truly lift your spirits, and subconsciously reduces stress. Have you ever walked into a hotel room, or stayed at a vrbo/air b&b? The place is simple and clean. Whether you realize it or not, your mind relaxes!

Another big reason to start sorting things out now? Eventually, someone will have to clean out your living space. When my mother passed unexpectedly, it was not just the grief that overwhelmed me, it was the mountain of stuff she left behind. What I thought would take a few weeks turned into months of sorting, donating, crying, and wondering why she kept so many cook books. It was exhausting, heartbreaking, and honestly, a little hilarious at times. Trust me, doing a little organizing now is one of the kindest gifts you can leave behind.

My father passed later in life, and had already gone through the downsizing process. It was still time consuming and distressing. I am sure no one wants to do this to our loved ones. We want to be remembered with love, not frustration and resentment. Keep that in mind as you look around your living space, and in those closets, basements, and garages. You could sell or donate what your loved ones do not want, and then your home will be a cozy place that will be simpler for you, less stress, and even more comfortable for your future visitors.

DOCUMENT

The following pages are to help others that may come in and need to take over. Nothing better than having a manual to ease your loved one's stress trying to figure these things out. Not only that, but as we get older, we forget who we used, we lose paperwork and information. When did I do this, or that? This is a great place to document and keep track of it all. A reference for not only you, but for anyone else that must take over if you cannot, or you pass. Again, the purpose for documenting this information is to reduce pain and stress for you as you age, and the people you love for down the road.

PROPERTY TAX

Another tip I would like to share with you regards Property tax. As a reminder, I have not researched every state, but something I suggest you look into. Many states and localities do offer some sort of discount or reduction of property taxes based on your age. There might be additional requirements such as income, estate values, and residency requirements. Please be aware that you might have to apply each year, and there might be deadlines for your application. Applying with your application does not automatically allow you to delay your payment. Check with your local town clerk or assessor.

Our local area offers additional savings at a certain age if you volunteer your time to the town. If possible, taking advantage of a bartering system is a great idea! Many seniors have more time than money and this is a great way to reduce some of those expenses.

Check with your utility companies, phone companies, and internet. You never know what possible discount you might be missing out on.

A. Type of Property (Residential, Rental, Commercial) _____

Address / Parcel No.: _____

Property Deeded to: _____

Mortgage holder: _____

Mortgage Account No. _____ Mortgage Balance: _____

Home Equity Line: Bank: _____ Total $ Amount: _____

Home Owners Association Contact: _____

Home Security Company: _____

Septic or Well: _____ Install Date: _____

Heat Type: Oil ____ Electric _____ Wood _____ Pellet _____ Mini Split _____ Propane _____

Cooling Type: Electric _____ Mini Split _____ Window Units _____

Beneficiary/s_____

Most Recent Repairs: Roof Date: _____ Hot Water Tank: _____ Other: _____

_____

_____

_____

(See Monthly Expenses for details)

Property Taxes: _____
　　　　　　　　　(Paid in Escrow or Paid to Town)　　(Account No.)

Property Insurance: _____
　　　　　　　　　　(Paid in Escrow or Paid to Ins.)　(Account No.)

Electricity Provider: _____
　　　　　　　　　　(Name)　　(Account No.)　　　　(URL)

Cable / Wi-Fi Co: _____
　　　　　　　　　(Name)　　(Account No.)　　　　(URL)

Gas Provider: _____
　　　　　　　(Name)　　(Account No.)　　　　(URL)

Oil/Propane Provider: _____
　　　　　　　　　　(Name)　　(Account No.)　　　　(URL)

Water Provider: _____
　　　　　　　　(Name)　　(Account No.)　　　　(URL)

NAME AND CONTACT OF REPAIR AND MAINTENANCE COMPANIES

Plumber: _____

Electrician: _____

HVAC: _____

Exterminator: _____

Appliance Repair: _____

Landscape Maint: _____

Oil / Propane Maint. Co. _____

Snow Plow Co.: _____

Generator Co: _____

Pool/Hot tub Co.: _____

Septic Co.: _____

Cleaning Co: _____

Trash Removal Co: _____

Other: _____

Other: _____

Other: _____

B.   Type of Property (Residential, Rental, Commercial) _____

Address / Parcel No.: _____

Property Deeded to: _____

Mortgage holder: _____

Mortgage Account No. _____ Mortgage Balance: _____

Home Equity Line: Bank: _____ Total $ Amount: _____

Home Owners Association Contact: _____

Home Security Company: _____

Septic or Well: _____ Install Date: _____

Heat Type: Oil ____ Electric _____ Wood _____ Pellet _____ Mini Split _____ Propane _____

Cooling Type: Electric _____ Mini Split _____ Window Units _____

Beneficiary/s_____

Most Recent Repairs: Roof Date: _____ Hot Water Tank: _____ Other: _____

_____

_____

_____

(See Monthly Expenses for details)

Property Taxes: _____
                      (Paid in Escrow or Paid to Town)   (Account No.)

Property Insurance: _____
                      (Paid in Escrow or Paid to Ins.)   (Account No.)

Electricity Provider: _____
                (Name)   (Account No.)   (URL)

Cable / Wi-Fi Co: _____
                (Name)   (Account No.)   (URL)

Gas Provider: _____
                (Name)   (Account No.)   (URL)

Oil/Propane Provider: _____
                (Name)   (Account No.)   (URL)

Water Provider: _____
                (Name)   (Account No.)   (URL)

NAME AND CONTACT OF REPAIR AND MAINTENANCE COMPANIES

Plumber: _____

Electrician: _____

HVAC: _____

Exterminator: _____

Appliance Repair: _____

Landscape Maint: _____

Oil / Propane Maint. Co. _____

Snow Plow Co.: _____

Generator Co: _____

Pool/Hot tub Co.: _____

Septic Co.: _____

Cleaning Co: _____

Trash Removal Co: _____

Other: _____

Other: _____

Other: _____

C.   Type of Property (Residential, Rental, Commercial) _____

Address / Parcel No.: _____

Property Deeded to: _____

Mortgage holder: _____

Mortgage Account No. _____ Mortgage Balance: _____

Home Equity Line: Bank: _____ Total $ Amount: _____

Home Owners Association Contact: _____

Home Security Company: _____

Septic or Well: _____ Install Date: _____

Heat Type: Oil ____ Electric _____ Wood _____ Pellet _____ Mini Split _____ Propane _____

Cooling Type: Electric _____ Mini Split _____ Window Units _____

Beneficiary/s_____

Most Recent Repairs: Roof Date: _____ Hot Water Tank: _____ Other: _____

_____

_____

_____

(See Monthly Expenses for details)

Property Taxes: _____
                    (Paid in Escrow or Paid to Town)   (Account No.)

Property Insurance: _____
                    (Paid in Escrow or Paid to Ins.)   (Account No.)

Electricity Provider: _____
                  (Name)   (Account No.)   (URL)

Cable / Wi-Fi Co: _____
                  (Name)   (Account No.)   (URL)

Gas Provider: _____
                  (Name)   (Account No.)   (URL)

Oil/Propane Provider: _____
                  (Name)   (Account No.)   (URL)

Water Provider: _____
                  (Name)   (Account No.)   (URL)

NAME AND CONTACT OF REPAIR AND MAINTENANCE COMPANIES

Plumber: _____

Electrician: _____

HVAC: _____

Exterminator: _____

Appliance Repair: _____

Landscape Maint: _____

Oil / Propane Maint. Co. _____

Snow Plow Co.: _____

Generator Co: _____

Pool/Hot tub Co.: _____

Septic Co.: _____

Cleaning Co: _____

Trash Removal Co: _____

Other: _____

Other: _____

Other: _____

STORAGE UNIT

Storage Company: _____
(ADDRESS)
_____
(Account No.)   (Unit #)   (Lock Combination / Key Location)   (Monthly Payment $ / Auto Payment Info)

Storage Company: _____
(ADDRESS)
_____
(Account No.)   (Unit #)   (Lock Combination / Key Location)   (Monthly Payment $ / Auto Payment Info)

SAFETY DEPOSIT BOX

Bank or Institution: _____
(Address)
_____
(Owner's Name)   (Other Name and Key Holder)   (Key Location)

_____
(Unit or Box No.)   (Monthly Payment $ / Auto Payment Info)

SAFE

Location: _____
(Address And Location)
_____
(Lock Combination or Key Location)

Location: _____
(Address And Location)
_____
(Lock Combination or Key Location)

ALL MY STUFF

This will not over ride your will or trust. However, there are items you may have that will not be listed out specifically. If you have something that you want specific people to have, then I advise you put it in your legal documents. Please attach a story to your item. It brings value to your loved ones. Write out the item, the story/history, and who should receive it.

This section can also be a way of organizing your "stuff" before visiting a lawyer to draw up your legal documents. It could be a recipe, a book, a ring, a photograph, or car!

*Item:*_____

_____

_____

*Item:*_____

_____

_____

*Item:*_____

_____

_____

*Item:*_____

_____

_____

*Item:*_____

_____

_____

*Item:*_____
_____
_____

*Item:*_____
_____
_____

*Item:*_____
_____
_____

*Item:*_____
_____
_____

*Item:*_____
_____
_____

*Item:*_____
_____
_____

*Item:*_____
_____
_____

*Item:*_____

_____

_____

*Item:*_____

_____

_____

*Item:*_____

_____

_____

*Item:*_____

_____

_____

*Item:*_____

_____

_____

*Item:*_____

_____

_____

*Item:*_____

_____

_____

Financial

- **Bank Accounts**

  - **CD's and Lockbox**

- **Other Types of Assets & Accounts**

  - **Treasury**

  - **Life Insurance**

  - **Disability Short and Long Term**

- **Investment Accounts**

- **Leaving Your IRA to Your Loved Ones**

- **Individual Stocks and Bonds**

- **Pensions**

FINANCIAL

DID YOU KNOW?

Adding your child to your bank account can be a smart thing to do to avoid problems or delays down the road. It could also help them manage your bills and expenses easier. A will or Trust will not override the directions on the cash account. This is exactly what we did with my dad's accounts, and it was seamless. Keep yourself as the primary account holder, and your child or loved one, the secondary. That is the upswing, but there is a potential down swing you need to be aware of.

Choosing the wrong person to manage your cash assets could be disastrous. Make sure that your chosen person is honest, has your best interest as the priority, and is financially responsible. The named person could withdrawal the entire balance, so having trust in this person is imperative. If you have chosen to split all your assets equally amongst your children, this account will not be visible to the trust. Communicating to your other heirs, that it is to be split equally, and having documents acknowledging this reduces potential problems.

If you have certificates, they can be cashed out early without penalty from your financial institution. Federal law prohibits them from charging early withdrawal penalties upon your death.

BANK ACCOUNTS

Name of Institution: _____

Address and Phone: _____

Bank Website: _____

Login: User Name _____ Password: _____

Account Type: Checking   Savings   Account No. _____

Account Type: Checking   Savings   Account No. _____

Account Type: Checking   Savings   Account No. _____

Account Type: Checking   Savings   Account No. _____

Lock Box: Box No. _____ Signers_____

Where is Key Located? _____

Certificates (CD's) _____ Date Opened and Due _____

Certificates (CD's) _____ Date Opened and Due _____

Name of Institution: _____

Address and Phone: _____

Bank Website: _____

Login: User Name _____ Password: _____

Account Type:	Checking	Savings	Account No. _____
Account Type:	Checking	Savings	Account No. _____
Account Type:	Checking	Savings	Account No. _____
Account Type:	Checking	Savings	Account No. _____

Lock Box: Box No. _____ Signers _____

Where is Key Located? _____

Certificates (CD's) _____ Date Opened and Due _____

Certificates (CD's) _____ Date Opened and Due _____

Certificates (CD's) _____ Date Opened and Due _____

Certificates (CD's) _____ Date Opened and Due _____

Name of Institution: _____

Address and Phone: _____

Bank Website: _____

Login: User Name _____ Password: _____

Account Type:	Checking	Savings	Account No. _____
Account Type:	Checking	Savings	Account No. _____
Account Type:	Checking	Savings	Account No. _____
Account Type:	Checking	Savings	Account No. _____

Lock Box: Box No. _____ Signers _____

Where is Key Located? _____

Certificates (CD's) _____ Date Opened and Due _____

Certificates (CD's) _____ Date Opened and Due _____

Certificates (CD's) _____ Date Opened and Due _____

Certificates (CD's) _____ Date Opened and Due _____

OTHER TYPES OF FINANCIAL ACCOUNTS AND ASSETS

This could include Savings Bonds, Treasury Bills, Flexible Spending accounts, Health savings accounts, educational savings accounts, and accounts you may be managing and listed as your asset. An example could be a 529 Educational account for your children and/or grandchildren.

LIFE INSURANCE

Name of Institution: _____

Address and Phone: _____

Bank Website: _____ Account No. _____

Login: User Name _____ Password: _____

Beneficiaries: _____

DISABILITY LONG TERM

Name of Institution: _____

Address and Phone: _____

Bank Website: _____ Account No. _____

Login: User Name _____ Password: _____

DISABILITY SHORT TERM

Name of Institution: _____

Address and Phone: _____

Bank Website: _____ Account No. _____

Login: User Name _____ Password: _____

LONG TERM CARE INSURANCE

Name of Institution: _____

Address and Phone: _____

Bank Website: _____ Account No. _____

Login: User Name _____ Password: _____

OTHER

Name of Institution: _____

Address and Phone: _____

Bank Website: _____ Account No. _____

Login: User Name _____ Password: _____

Beneficiaries: _____

Name of Institution: _____

Address and Phone: _____

Bank Website: _____ Account No. _____

Login: User Name _____ Password: _____

Beneficiaries: _____

Name of Institution: _____

Address and Phone: _____

Bank Website: _____ Account No. _____

Login: User Name _____ Password: _____

Beneficiaries: _____

Name of Institution: _____

Address and Phone: _____

Bank Website: _____ Account No. _____

Login: User Name _____ Password: _____

Beneficiaries: _____

Name of Institution: _____

Address and Phone: _____

Bank Website: _____ Account No. _____

Login: User Name _____ Password: _____

Beneficiaries: _____

INVESTMENT ACCOUNTS

DID YOU KNOW?

Naming a Beneficiary on your accounts supersedes any designation listed on your will or trust. It is a good idea to periodically verify who is listed as your primary beneficiary with a secondary beneficiary in the event you outlive your primary. Most banks and institutions will allow several names with percentages for each. Take all of this into account when putting your estate plan together.

I am going to share some very important guidance with you regarding your investment accounts, and if I could scream it from the roof tops, I would!

The scenario – You have done everything **right**, designated all your assets, set up savings accounts, purchased all the right insurances, filled out every document. Crossed every "T," dotted every "I." You have your IRA invested with a certain brokerage company and things are running smoothly while you are in charge. You are collecting your RMD's (Required Minimum Distribution), and life is fine.

1st Potential Problem – You have a limited amount of cash, and then the need for supplemental care arises. This is care that either is not covered by insurance or, worse, you do not have any insurance at all. You might think you have enough family to pitch in and care for you, but let's be honest — we do not have a crystal ball. How do we know that family will be there when needed? And, let's face it, even if they are, they might need help themselves.

You think you have planned ahead. You have saved in your 401(k) or IRA, and you are ready for whatever comes your way. Everything is fine, right? Well… maybe. But it could also go sideways.

Depending on your brokerage firm, and the type of accounts you have, it could take weeks, even months, to access your funds. You assume, when you need a distribution (some of **your** money) now to pay someone or settle a bill, having to wait while your brokerage firm shuffles papers, is more than just frustrating, it is a serious problem. And you cannot just swipe a credit card or make a quick transfer. Picture the stress and chaos that builds up when you cannot access what you need in a timely manner.

2nd Potential Problem – You have done everything right. You have put all your assets into a trust, worked with a reputable attorney, and set everything up for your beneficiaries. But when it is time to distribute your estate, the brokerage firm that holds your IRA or pension starts to what feels like "playing games".

Brokerage firms are not in a hurry to distribute funds. In fact, they are experts at dragging their feet. Your beneficiaries could be drowning in mountains of legal paperwork, filled with jargon that requires signatures, notarization, and endless back-and-forth. What is worse, this process could take months, even up to a year in some cases. Some brokerage firms can drag their heels, all while charging ridiculous fees. I can think of a particular firm that I hear about over and over. Now that I know about this, it is enough to make you spit fire.

Do your homework. Check with your firm to understand exactly how your accounts will be handled in these scenarios. Do not let your beneficiaries be caught in the middle of the financial version of a maze.

Both situations happened to us. Personally, I work with a top brokerage firm that I am very happy with. I can manage my investments online, and transfers or changes can be made quickly — from 24 hours to just a few days, not weeks or months. Plus, I can call them at any time and set up a face-to-face meeting whenever I need it.

My dad, however, used a brokerage firm that was offered through his employer. Like many of us, that is how he started his retirement savings. But the firm he worked with, which handles millions of accounts, made it nearly impossible to access his funds in a timely manner, both when he was alive, and after he passed. Without getting into specifics, I will just say that the process was so frustrating and slow that it felt like we were stuck in a never-ending loop of paperwork.

We quickly brought in my dad's attorney to help us navigate their drawn-out process. You should not have to involve an attorney just to access your inherited retirement funds. This company, which handles countless retirement accounts, has an incredibly slow and difficult process for beneficiaries to deal with. Despite filing a formal complaint multiple times, our concerns were ignored.

I cannot stress this enough; Research the company holding your retirement funds. Make sure you understand their processes and timelines, get it in writing. My father's situation is one that many seniors like him unknowingly face. Imagine grieving the loss of a loved one, only to then deal with a slow and unresponsive financial institution. It is an emotional toll that should not be part of the process. *Okay... let me breathe for a second... I still have PTSD from it!*

LEAVING YOUR IRA TO YOUR LOVED ONES

Once you pass your heirs will inherit your balances. But what you may not know is that the government changed the laws in 2020. Pre 2020, heirs could withdrawal inherited IRAs over their lifetime. The new law, **"The Secure Act,"** heirs must withdrawal the entire amount over the course of **ten years**. The reason this is important is because this could change your heirs' tax bracket. This rule does not apply to spouses, but does apply to non-spousal beneficiaries. It does not apply to minor children, (minors have a special rule that applies once minors reach the age of maturity) disabled or chronically ill beneficiaries, and certain trusts. It also does not apply to beneficiaries who are within 10-years of the age of the original account holder.

*If you do not follow these rules, you could face a 50% penalty on any remaining money in the account. You could take it all out at once, or spread it out over 10-years, either way, it must be depleted within 10-years. If your beneficiary passes before those 10-years, the 10-year clock does not restart. Their beneficiary will have the same date as the original heir. All funds based on date of death of the original investor. I wish I could put a big eyeball emoji here.

If you plan to pass on an IRA to a loved one or are in a position to inherit one, here are some things to consider to help make matters easier down the road.

IF THE MONEY IS IN A TRUST

In some cases, an inherited IRA may be kept in a trust. This can complicate things for younger beneficiaries who may not have access to the trust until they are a certain age or may only be allowed to withdraw a certain amount of money each year. If you plan to have a trust listed as the beneficiary of your IRA, you may want to adapt your planning to factor these recent changes. For example, you could structure your IRA so that funds from the account are evenly distributed over each of the 10 years. This way, your beneficiaries would not have to withdraw all the money at one time, which may result in a larger tax bill. You also could consider using a different type of trust, such as an accumulation or discretionary trust, that may offer more flexibility to either distribute or retain funds within the account. However, this will come with certain tax consequences, so it may be helpful to talk to an estate planning attorney to determine an appropriate strategy for your needs.

SPREADING OUT DISTRIBUTIONS

Because of the new 10-year rule, there are no longer any RMD requirements for non-spousal beneficiaries who do not fall into one of the exceptions. However, if you inherit an IRA in the coming years, and you do not meet one of the exceptions to the 10-year rule, you could take equal distributions to help spread out your tax liability over the 10 years. You also could take larger distributions during the years your income is lower. Because a lower income could lower your tax bracket, and reduce the tax liability. Again, the right option for you will depend on your unique situation. Consider speaking with a tax professional for more information.

ANNUITIES

Another option is to convert the assets in the IRA into an annuity. An annuity could help defer taxes, offer growth potential, and help set up an income stream that meets the 10-year requirement.

If you are the original IRA account holder and have already converted your IRA into an annuity, you can pass this on to your beneficiaries. If you have already started to receive payments from the annuity, the insurance company may give your beneficiaries a refund of the unpaid premium after your death — depending on your policy.

ROTH CONVERSIONS

If you have a traditional IRA, you could also convert it to a Roth IRA and pay the taxes on the amount you convert. If certain qualifications are met, this may allow your beneficiaries to withdraw distributions over 10 years without having to pay taxes. However, this approach may come with certain fees and tax consequences, so consider talking to financial professional or tax expert or attorney to best decide what is best for your situation.

MANAGING AN INHERITED IRA FOR THE FUTURE

Leaving loved ones, a financial legacy can be very important for many parents, spouses, and grandparents. Whether you intend to pass on an IRA or expect to inherit one, it can be helpful to understand how the new 10-year rule may affect you. Consider talking to the right financial professionals as you navigate these changes. If we had personally known about this law change, we would have done things differently.

The following section is where you document all your IRA's, 401ks, all your retirements and investments. It is a good time to review where your funds are at, how they are performing, and maybe consolidate. Meeting with a financial advisor can help you do just that; especially if you are unsure or not a savvy investor. Please make sure all your financial institutions have the appropriate beneficiaries listed.

Name of Institution: _____

Address and Phone: _____

Brokerage Website: _____

Login: User Name _____ Password: _____

Name of account manager / bank / broker _____

There are many types of accounts; and you probably have several. List them here:

Account Type: _____ Account No. _____
Beneficiary: _____

Account Type: _____ Account No. _____
Beneficiary: _____

Account Type: _____ Account No. _____
Beneficiary: _____

Account Type: _____ Account No. _____
Beneficiary: _____

Account Type: _____ Account No. _____
Beneficiary: _____

Account Type: _____ Account No. _____
Beneficiary: _____

Account Type: _____ Account No. _____

Beneficiary: _____

— · — · — · — · — · — · — · — · — · — · — · — · — · — · — · — · —

Name of Institution: _____

Address and Phone: _____

Brokerage Website: _____

Login: User Name _____ Password: _____

Name of account manager / bank / broker _____

There are many types of accounts; and you probably have several. List them here:

Account Type: _____ Account No. _____

Beneficiary: _____

Account Type: _____ Account No. _____

Beneficiary: _____

Account Type: _____ Account No. _____

Beneficiary: _____

Account Type: _____ Account No. _____

Beneficiary: _____

Account Type: _____ Account No. _____

Beneficiary: _____

Account Type: _____ Account No. _____

Beneficiary: _____

Account Type: _____ Account No. _____

Beneficiary: _____

— · — · — · — · — · — · — · — · — · — · — · — · — · — · — · — · —

Name of Institution: _____

Address and Phone: _____

Brokerage Website: _____

Login: User Name _____ Password: _____

Name of account manager / bank / broker _____

There are many types of accounts; and you probably have several. List them here:

Account Type: _____ Account No. _____

Beneficiary: _____

Account Type: _____ Account No. _____

Beneficiary: _____

Account Type: _____ Account No. _____

Beneficiary: _____

Account Type: _____ Account No. _____

Beneficiary: _____

Account Type: _____ Account No. _____

Beneficiary: _____

Account Type: _____ Account No. _____

Beneficiary: _____

Account Type: _____ Account No. _____

Beneficiary: _____

INDIVIDUAL STOCKS AND BONDS

Name of Institution: _____

Address and Phone: _____

Brokerage Website: _____

Login: User Name _____ Password: _____

Name of account manager / bank / broker _____

Name of Stock or Bond: _____

Description: _____

CUSIP No. _____ Number of Shares: _____

Location of Certificate: _____

Name of Stock or Bond: _____

Description: _____

CUSIP No. _____ Number of Shares: _____

Location of Certificate: _____

Name of Stock or Bond: _____

Description: _____

CUSIP No. _____ Number of Shares: _____

Location of Certificate: _____

Name of Stock or Bond: _____

Description: _____

CUSIP No. _____ Number of Shares: _____

Location of Certificate: _____

Name of Stock or Bond: _____

Description: _____

CUSIP No. _____ Number of Shares: _____

Location of Certificate: _____

PENSIONS

Type of Pension: _____

Name of Institution: _____

Address and Phone: _____

Name of Account Holder / Plan participant _____

Website: _____

Login: User Name _____ Password: _____

Email address: _____

Name of account manager or Employer Plan Contact: _____

Type of Pension: _____

Name of Institution: _____

Address and Phone: _____

Name of Account Holder / Plan participant _____

Website: _____

Login: User Name _____ Password: _____

Email address: _____

Name of account manager or Employer Plan Contact: _____

Monthly Financial Overview

- ❖ **Monthly Income: Government Benefits**

- ❖ **Monthly Income: Other Sources**

- ❖ **Expenses and Liabilities**

  - ○ **Monthly Creditors**

  - ○ **Debts and Liabilities**

MONTHLY FINANCIAL OVERVIEW

DID YOU KNOW?

Once you pass away, any monthly amounts paid from a state or federal resource, will be rescinded for the month you have passed, and going forward. If they are direct deposited, they will be withdrawn. If you are a Veteran, check with the local veteran's office, you may be intitled for some death benefits. If someone owes you funds, please document under, "Other Source"

MONTHLY INCOME: GOVERNMENT BENEFITS

Social Security: Account No._____ Amount: $ _____

_____
(Online ID)   *(Password)*   *(Local Office Location/Phone)*

Automatic Deposit or Mail: _____ Account Deposited to: _____

Medicare/Medicaid: Account No._____ Amount: $ _____

_____
(Online ID)   *(Password)*   *(Local Office Location/Phone)*

Automatic Deposit or Mail: _____ Account Deposited to: _____

Veteran Pension: Account No._____ Amount: $ _____

_____
(Online ID)   *(Password)*   *(Local Office Location/Phone)*

Automatic Deposit or Mail: _____ Account Deposited to: _____

Gov't Pension: Account No._____ Amount: $ _____

_____
(Online ID)   *(Password)*   *(Local Office Location/Phone)*

Automatic Deposit or Mail: _____ Account Deposited to: _____

Other Pension: Account No._____   Amount: $ _____

_____
(Online ID)   (Password)   (Local Office Location/Phone)

Automatic Deposit or Mail: _____ Account Deposited to: _____

MONTHLY INCOME: OTHER SOURCES

Source: _____ Account No./ID _____

_____
(Name)   (Address)   (Phone)   (Email)

Amount: $ _____   Frequency: _____

Automatic Deposit or Mail: _____ Account Deposited to: _____

Source: _____   Account No./ID _____

_____
(Name)   (Address)   (Phone)   (Email)

Amount: $ _____   Frequency: _____

Automatic Deposit or Mail: _____ Account Deposited to: _____

Source: _____ Account No./ID _____

_____
(Name)   (Address)   (Phone)   (Email)

Amount: $ _____   Frequency: _____

Automatic Deposit or Mail: _____ Account Deposited to: _____

EXPENSES AND LIABILITIES

DID YOU KNOW?

Many of your providers will not speak to anyone else other than you. For example, I tried to reduce my father's cable bill; we no longer needed the package he had. They would not speak to me, and drilled me like I was robbing his bank accounts! It infuriated me! Having a family member in their notes that can make changes, reduce or cancel services, will save frustration!

MONTHLY CREDITORS:

Electricity Provider: _____
                (Name)   *(Account No.)*   *(URL)*

_____
(User Name)   *(Password)*   *(Auto Payment/ Check)*   *(Bank)*

Cable / Wi-Fi Co: _____
                (Name)   *(Account No.)*   *(URL)*

_____
(User Name)   *(Password)*   *(Auto Payment/ Check)*   *(Bank)*

Heat Provider: _____
                (Name)   *(Account No.)*   *(URL)*

_____
(User Name)   *(Password)*   *(Auto Payment/ Check)*   *(Bank)*

Oil/Propane Provider: _____
                (Name)   *(Account No.)*   *(URL)*

_____
(User Name)   *(Password)*   *(Auto Payment/ Check)*   *(Bank)* *(Auto-Fill Frequency)*

Water Provider: _____
                (Name)   *(Account No.)*   *(URL)*

_____
(User Name)   *(Password)*   *(Auto Payment/ Check)*   *(Bank)*

Cell Phone Provider: _____
                (Name)   *(Account No.)*   *(URL)*

_____
(User Name)   *(Password)*   *(Auto Payment/ Check)*   *(Bank)*

Rent: Amount: $ _____

(Name)	(Account No.)	(URL)

(Address of Landlord)

(User Name)　　(Password)　　(Auto Payment/ Check)　　(Bank)

Other Type: Amount: $ _____

(Name)　　(Account No.)　　(URL)

(User Name)　　(Password)　　(Auto Payment/ Check)　　(Bank)

Other Type: Amount: $ _____

(Name)　　(Account No.)　　(URL)

(User Name)　　(Password)　　(Auto Payment/ Check)　　(Bank)

Other Type: Amount: $ _____

(Name)　　(Account No.)　　(URL)

(User Name)　　(Password)　　(Auto Payment/ Check)　　(Bank)

Other Type: Amount: $ _____

(Name)　　(Account No.)　　(URL)

(User Name)　　(Password)　　(Auto Payment/ Check)　　(Bank)

Other Type: Amount: $ _____

(Name)　　(Account No.)　　(URL)

(User Name)　　(Password)　　(Auto Payment/ Check)　　(Bank)

Other Type: Amount: $ _____

(Name)　　(Account No.)　　(URL)

(User Name)　　(Password)　　(Auto Payment/ Check)　　(Bank)

DEBTS AND LIABILITIES

HOMES 🏠 RENTALS

Primary Home Mortgage: Address: _____

_____
(Name)   (Account No.)   (URL)

_____
(User Name)   (Password)   (Auto Payment/ Check)   (Bank)

Property Tax: _____
(Name)   (Account No.)   (URL)

_____
(User Name)   (Password)   (Auto Payment/ Check)   (Bank)

Home Owners Ins: _____
(Name)   (Account No.)   (URL)

_____
(User Name)   (Password)   (Auto Payment/ Check)   (Bank)

Equity Line: Address: _____

_____
(Name)   (Account No.)   (URL)

_____
(User Name)   (Password)   (Auto Payment/ Check)   (Bank)

Secondary Property Mortgage: Address: _____

_____
(Name)   (Account No.)   (URL)

_____
(User Name)   (Password)   (Auto Payment/ Check)   (Bank)

Property Tax: _____
(Name)   (Account No.)   (URL)

_____
(User Name)   (Password)   (Auto Payment/ Check)   (Bank)

Home Owners Ins: _____
(Name)   (Account No.)   (URL)

_____
(User Name)   (Password)   (Auto Payment/ Check)   (Bank)

Equity Line: Address: _____

_____
                          (Name)   *(Account No.)*   *(URL)*

_____
(User Name)   *(Password)*   *(Auto Payment/ Check)*   *(Bank)*

Rental Property Mortgage:

Address: _____

_____
                          (Name)   *(Account No.)*   *(URL)*

_____
(User Name)   *(Password)*   *(Auto Payment / Check)*   *(Bank)*

Property Tax: _____
                          (Name)   *(Account No.)*   *(URL)*

_____
(User Name)   *(Password)*   *(Auto Payment / Check)*   *(Bank)*

Home Owners Ins:

_____
                          (Name)   *(Account No.)*   *(URL)*

_____
(User Name)   *(Password)*   *(Auto Payment / Check)*   *(Bank)*

CREDIT 💳 CARDS

Credit Card: _____
                          (Name)   *(Account No.)*   *(URL)*

_____
(User Name)   *(Password)*   *(Auto Payment / Check)*   *(Bank)*

Credit Card: _____
                          (Name)   *(Account No.)*   *(URL)*

_____
(User Name)   *(Password)*   *(Auto Payment / Check)*   *(Bank)*

Credit Card: _____
                          (Name)   *(Account No.)*   *(URL)*

_____
(User Name)   *(Password)*   *(Auto Payment / Check)*   *(Bank)*

VEHICLES

1. **Vehicle Loan:**

   _____
   (Name)   (Account No.)   (URL)

   _____
   (User Name)   (Password)   (Amount Auto Payment/ Check)   (Bank)

   _____
   (Year)   (Make and Model)   (Total Amount of Loan)

2. **Vehicle Loan:**

   _____
   (Name)   (Account No.)   (URL)

   _____
   (User Name)   (Password)   (Amount Auto Payment/ Check)   (Bank)

   _____
   (Year)   (Make and Model)   (Total Amount of Loan)

3. **Vehicle Loan:**

   _____
   (Name)   (Account No.)   (URL)

   _____
   (User Name)   (Password)   (Amount Auto Payment/ Check)   (Bank)

   _____
   (Year)   (Make and Model)   (Total Amount of Loan)

EQUIPMENT TRAILERS / YARD

1. **Equipment Loan:**

   _____
   (Name)   (Account No.)   (URL)

   _____
   (User Name)   (Password)   (Amount Auto Payment/ Check)   (Bank)

   _____
   (Year)   (Make and Model)   (Total Amount of Loan)

2. **Equipment Loan:**

_____
(Name)   (Account No.)   (URL)

_____
(User Name)   (Password)   (Amount Auto Payment/ Check)   (Bank)

_____
(Year)   (Make and Model)   (Total Amount of Loan)

PERSONAL

Personal Loan: _____
                 (Name of Lender)   (Account No.)   (URL)

_____
(User Name)   (Password)   (Amount Auto Payment / Check)   (Bank)

Other Type Loan: _____
                    (Name of Lender)   (Account No.)   (URL)

_____
(User Name)   (Password)   (Amount Auto Payment/ Check)   (Bank)

Other Type Debt: _____
                    (Name)   (Account No.)   (URL)

_____
(User Name)   (Password)   (Amount Auto Payment/ Check)   (Bank)

Other Type Debt: _____
                    (Name)   (Account No.)   (URL)

_____
(User Name)   (Password)   (Amount Auto Payment/ Check)   (Bank)

Safety Deposit Lock Box

_____
                 (Name)   (Account No.)   (URL)

_____
(User Name)   (Password)   (Amount Auto Payment/ Check)   (Bank)

My Legal Information & Important Documents

- ❖ **Contact Information and Location of My Legal Documents**
    - Power of Attorney
    - Healthcare Proxy
    - Attorney
    - Executor
    - Will/Trust
    - Military Documents
    - Birth Certificate
    - Passport and Driver's License
    - Marriage / Divorce Documents
- ❖ **Power of Attorney and Healthcare Proxy**
    - Types and Their Responsibilities

LEGAL INFORMATION & IMPORTANT DOCUMENTS

WHO IS MY LEGAL CONTACT

Where are your legal documents located? Who has possession? Are they in a Bank lockbox? These documents are super important. Having them done is a hurdle, but if the person handling your estate has no idea where they are, it does no good.

In this section we are going to document where they are, and who you have assigned to manage it. My mother past at a young age, and as her children we knew she had a will, but had no idea who did it, and where it was. This haunts me to this day. Everything we did from planning her funeral, to managing her home, was a guess. Filling out this page will save your descendants and loved ones these challenges.

Healthcare Proxy: _____

Power of Attorney: _____

Attorney: _____

Executor: _____

If these documents are in a bank or held by someone you trust, **Who and Where are they located**?

Do you have a Will or Trust? Who has copies and Where

(Name)	(Address)	(Phone)	(Email)
(Name)	(Address)	(Phone)	(Email)
(Name)	(Address)	(Phone)	(Email)

Who is your Tax Accountant? Where are your Tax Returns?

(Name)	(Address)	(Phone)	(Email)

MY MAIN DOCUMENTS

Driver's License No. _____ Passport Location _____

Birth Certificate Location: _____ Social Security: _____

Marriage Certificate: _____

Divorce Documents: _____

Veterans Documents: DD214 Location _____

Pension Information _____ Veteran Contact Info: _____

Other: _____

Other: _____

Other: _____

Other: _____

INCOME RECEIPTS

Total Monthly Amount: $ _____ Annual $: _____

Automatic Deposit or Mail: _____ Deposited to: _____

MILITARY RECORDS

Branch of Service: _____ Highest Rank: _____ Date of Service: _____

Pension Amount: $ _____ Dates of Service: _____

Automatic Deposit or Mail: _____ Account Deposited to: _____

    It is important to mention that if you do not have a certified copy of your **DD214** or **birth certificate** in your possession, then you need to get it! You can call the local town hall of the town you were born in, and contact your local veteran's office if you need a copy of your DD214. If you have got all your final financial documents completed, then Good for You! Having done this can give such a peace of mind. However, if you have not, then it is time to do so! Do not beat yourself up with any thoughts of… "I should have done this…" or "I wish I had done that…" The fact you are here at this point is fantastic, and your loved ones will be very appreciative!

Some of these documents can be very confusing, and their language even more so. Some people avoid the overwhelming task all together. Let us break it all down, and get it done together!

WHO IS IN CHARGE

Deciding who will have Power of Attorney or be your Executor could affect family dynamics for years to come. That person will oversee major decisions, both medical and financial. Even if you plan while you are fit and healthy, it can still cause problems in the family dynamic if not handled carefully.

In some families, it may be obvious who the Power of Attorney role should go to. It may be the oldest child, or it may be the child who lives closest, has a business mind, or understands the deepest details of your life. Maybe it is not your children at all, but you need to nominate who you think will always have your best mental and financial interest as the priority. Financial responsibility is obviously very important when it comes to who will handle the finances.

This decision has the potential to cause resistance or conflict from other children who may feel insulted. There are states that allow more than one per person to be Power of Attorney, check your state laws. However, this could cause issues down the line as well, especially if not everyone agrees on how a certain situation should be handled. There are also states where an individual can be named POA in specific areas. For example, one person may handle health care decisions, and another may handle financial decisions. It is logical to assign these separate roles to the children who have the most experience in them. There may be a doctor or nurse in the family who would oversee health care or family member in business or finance who understands that area better.

COMMUNICATION

Once you have made your choice, to reduce any potential family turmoil, communicate it! It might not be possible to do so with everyone in the same room; Using zoom, or meeting in an attorney's office could be alternative locations. Most of the time this goes very smooth, but not all families get along, and maybe it needs to be done separately. Maybe you have children that are estranged. If this is the case, it might be a good idea that you write them a letter explaining your reasons. This would be something they could retrieve before or after you have passed, but at least it might reduce animosity between siblings, after you are gone. Remember, the more you communicate, the higher the chances your loved ones will not pursue further legal action, or hold on to resentment after you are gone.

I have seen families be torn apart, and sibling rivalry can turn horrible quickly. A jealous or untrusting sibling may hound the POA sibling about their decisions which causes many drawn-out arguments and resentment. Communication with all parties about the duties of the Power of Attorney should be clearly laid out. If this is done ahead of time, your legacy and love for your family may stay in tacked.

The person who holds Power of Attorney **MUST** have your best interest. They must act on behalf of the person they are representing and do what is right for you. If other siblings feel it is not right, then that POA holder can be sued at a later date. A good example of this is when the living will states that there is to be no long-term life support. The POA may honor that, but other siblings refuse to let go of the dying parent, and it could cause a huge battle. No one wants to let go of their loved one, but the POA has the responsibility to carry out the wishes that are stated in the living will. Okay, now let's break that down a little deeper.

LONG TERM LIFE SUPPORT

Clearly *defining* what ***long-term life*** support means to you is essential, as your interpretation may differ from that of your loved ones. This became evident in our own family, despite how close we are. My father was clear, he did not want long-term life support. And like many, I believe most of us feel the same when we are healthy and living our daily lives. However, none of us truly know when or how our final moments will come, and what we believe in one stage of life may shift when we are in that moment, and facing that reality.

Let me briefly share with you why I believe it is important to be clear. In our situation, I was his primary caregiver, and there were multiple times when he needed short-term medical care. Those words — **short-term care** versus **long-term life support** — matter! It is important to be precise when discussing your wishes with family because there is a difference between life-sustaining treatment and being kept alive indefinitely by machines**.**

I was able to demonstrate to my siblings that I was honoring his current wishes, and I am forever grateful that they placed their trust in both me, and him, in that decision.

Yes, the decision only delayed the inevitable, but during that time, something truly special happened. My father had the chance to meet his newly born great-grandchild, experiencing the joy of holding the next generation in his arms. He also had one last opportunity to go fishing; his greatest passion. The smile on his face and the light in his eyes brought us all immense comfort, helping us find peace in the midst of saying goodbye.

POWER OF ATTORNEY AND HEALTHCARE PROXY

Navigating the Financial Aspects of Choosing a POA and Healthcare Proxy –

Inheritance can be a major source of conflict within families, sometimes leading to long-lasting divisions and even legal battles whether before or after your passing. One common issue arises when a child designated as Power of Attorney (POA) compensates themselves for caregiving expenses, such as doctor visits, medication management, and food. This can lead to disputes, especially if they believe their contributions entitle them to more than an equal share of the inheritance, despite prior agreements.

You should also put this information in writing. Clear and open communication with your children is essential, but documenting your decisions ensures there is little room for misunderstanding. While these conversations may be difficult, they help prevent future family conflicts and resentment. Talking about your wishes is important, but putting them in black and white minimizes ambiguity, reducing the risk of legal disputes or lingering animosity within the family.

Let's review some differences between the types of Power of Attorney documents you will most likely need. Arming yourself with information, will save you time and money.

TYPES OF (POA) POWER OF ATTORNEY

Durable Power Of Attorney: *A power of attorney that continues to be effective even if the principal (you) loses capacity.*

A **Durable Power of Attorney (DPOA)** is a legal document that grants someone the authority to manage your financial, legal, and healthcare affairs on your behalf. It is typically established in preparation for potential incapacity or when facing a progressive illness. This document includes clear safeguards to ensure that critical decisions can be made on your behalf, and in your best interest. The powers granted through a DPOA can cover a wide range of financial matters, including buying or selling real estate, handling bank transactions, making investments, and managing other assets. The extent of these powers is entirely at the discretion of you, known as the principal.

While the designated agent has the right to act on your behalf, their authority is subject to any limitations you specify in the document. Additionally, the agent's power ceases upon the principal's death unless they are explicitly named as the executor in the last will.

General Power Of Attorney: *A power of attorney that allows the agent (the person you choose) to make financial and healthcare choices for the principal (you) without the principal's consent.*

A **Power of Attorney (POA)** is a legal document that allows you (the principal) to give another person (the agent) the authority to act on your behalf. This means the agent can manage your finances, investments, healthcare decisions, and even represent you in legal matters, depending on the level of authority you grant them. You can choose to give them full control or limit their powers to specific tasks.

Having a POA in place can provide peace of mind, especially in the event of an accident or illness. If something happens and you are unable to handle your financial affairs, your designated agent can step in to pay bills, manage accounts, sign legal documents, and make business decisions as outlined in the POA. This ensures that your affairs continue to be managed smoothly without your direct involvement.

A Special Power Of Attorney: *This is a POA used for a specific time or situation.*

A **Special Power of Attorney (POA)** is a legal document that allows you to give someone permission to handle specific tasks on your behalf. This can be helpful when you are unable to be present to take care of important matters, such as closing a real estate deal or managing a business transaction.

This type of POA is also useful if you become temporarily unable to manage your affairs due to illness or injury. A **Limited POA** is a legally binding document that gives someone authority to act for you within the specific limits you set. This ensures that your interests are protected while allowing trusted individuals to handle important tasks when you cannot.

Key Difference:
A General POA ends if you become incapacitated, while a Durable POA remains valid and allows your agent to continue managing your affairs when you can no longer do so. The Special POA is for a specific task

HOW TO CHOOSE A POWER OF ATTORNEY – YOUR AGENT

Qualities to consider:

- Someone who can be trusted and will look out for your needs
- Someone that has done a respectable job in their own life with their financials
- Someone who can make tough choices
- Someone faithful to your requests regardless of others' opinions
- Someone who lives close to you or has flexibility to take care of your business
- If this is not a family member; always verify multiple forms of identification

State law will specify that the agent:

- Depending on state law, must be at least 18 years old.
- Cannot serve as the principal's primary care provider (regular doctor).

Things you cannot do with Power of Attorney:

- Write a will for them or edit their current will.
- Take money directly from their bank accounts.
- Make decisions after the person you are representing dies.
- Give away your role as agent in the power of attorney.

Banks and doctors will only recognize an agent's power to act when they are presented with the original power of attorney document. Therefore, it is important to keep track of your signed power of attorney. Deliver signed copies to each nominated agent as well as a copy of your Healthcare Power of Attorney to your healthcare provider.

You can cancel a Power Of Attorney at any time, as long as you have been deemed as having the mental capacity. The power of attorney must be canceled in writing, and any financial or other institutions that may have relied on it must be informed. Also inform the agent in writing that you are taking away the power to act on your behalf.

HEALTHCARE PROXY

A Health Care Proxy is a legal document that allows you to appoint someone you trust to make medical decisions on your behalf if you are unable to do so.

If you become unconscious, mentally incapacitated, or otherwise unable to communicate your medical wishes, your health care agent will step in and make decisions based on your preferences. These decisions can include treatment options, surgeries, life-support choices, and end-of-life care. Your agent is legally required to follow your wishes as stated in the document or, if your wishes are unclear, to make decisions based on your best interests.

Last Words

- **Notes to Loved Ones**
- **Apologies**

LAST WORDS

Notes to Loved ones:

Notes to Loved ones:

Apologies:

Additional Notes:

ACKNOWLEDGMENTS

I want to express my deepest gratitude to my loving and supportive husband—the one who patiently stands by my side, effortlessly picks up any balls I may drop, and never fails to make me laugh. With you by my side, every challenge can be overcome.

To my son and his wife, whom I proudly call daughter, and to the four beautiful grandchildren they have blessed me with, you are my greatest joy. In each of you, I see the spirit, intelligence, and love of my remarkable parents and grandparents, a legacy that continues to shine through.

I am also profoundly grateful for my dearest friends, whose love and encouragement have lifted me up and inspired me to reach for the stars. Your support has been a guiding light on life's journey, and I cherish each—and—every one of you.

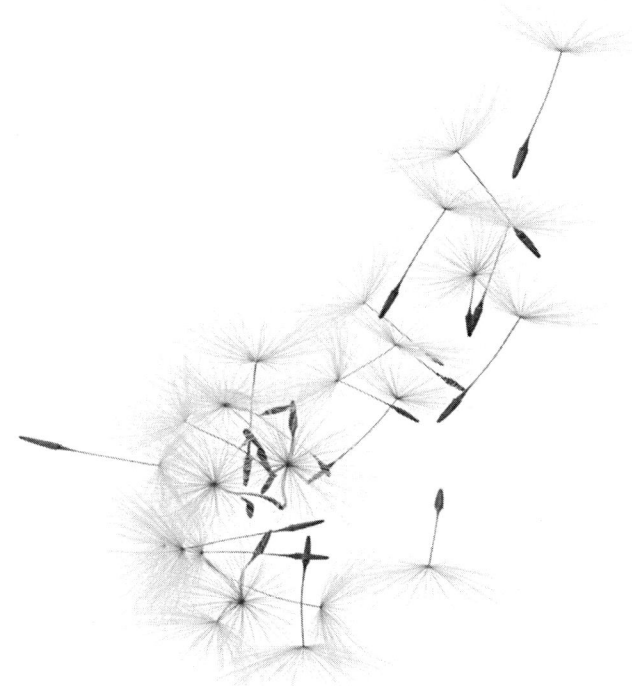

ABOUT THE AUTHOR

For over 25 years, C.J. Shearer built a successful career in finance, rising to the role of Chief Financial Officer. However, a personal health crisis in 2013 reshaped her perspective. After facing a cancer scare, she embraced a new path—entrepreneurship. Launching a thriving dog care business that combined her passion for animals with her desire for independence.

Beyond her career, C.J. Shearer has been deeply committed to her community. As Vice Chair of her town's *Finance Committee*, she assists in shaping its financial future, and through *Enhancing Shirley*, a town initiative she founded, she fosters pride, unity, and growth.

One of the most profound and personal roles in her life was becoming the primary caregiver for her father. What began as occasional assistance quickly evolved into a full-time responsibility. Managing his medical needs, ensuring his comfort, and striving to bring him joy was both a challenge and a privilege. Through this experience, she gained firsthand insight into the emotional, physical, and logistical struggles caregivers face. The overwhelming search for resources, the uncertainty of each decision, and the relentless effort to provide the best care inspired her to share her knowledge. Her hope is to help others navigate this journey with more confidence and support.

While her professional and community contributions are significant, her greatest joy comes from family. She is a devoted wife, mother, and grandmother, cherishing the laughter and love of her four grandchildren. Their innocence serves as a daily reminder of life's fragility and beauty.

Guided by her Christian faith, she has dedicated her life to serving others—whether through caregiving, leadership, or simply being a source of support. Her journey has been filled with challenges and triumphs, but above all, gratitude. She believes true fulfillment comes from making a difference, and she looks forward to continuing a life of purpose, service, and love.